Foul Deeds and ᴄᴜᴏᴜs Deaths Around Folkestone and Dover

FOUL DEEDS AND SUSPICIOUS DEATHS Series

Wharncliffe's *Foul Deeds and Suspicious Deaths* series explores, in detail, crimes of passion, brutal murders and foul misdemeanours from early modern times to the present day. Victorian street crime, mysterious death and modern murders tell tales where passion, jealousy and social deprivation brought unexpected violence to those involved. From unexplained death and suicide to murder and manslaughter, the books provide a fascinating insight into the lives of both victims and perpetrators as well as society as a whole.

Other titles in the series include:

Foul Deeds and Suspicious Deaths in Birmingham, Nick Billingham
ISBN: 1-903425-96-4. £10.99

Foul Deeds and Suspicious Deaths in Bolton, Glynis Cooper
ISBN: 1-903425-63-8. £9.99

Foul Deeds and Suspicious Deaths in Colchester, Patrick Denney
ISBN: 1-903425-80-8. £10.99

Foul Deeds and Suspicious Deaths in Coventry, David McGrory
ISBN: 1-903425-57-3. £9.99

Foul Deeds and Suspicious Deaths Around Derby, Kevin Turton
ISBN: 1-903425-76-X. £9.99

Foul Deeds and Suspicious Deaths in and around Durham, Maureen Anderson
ISBN: 1-903425-46-8. £9.99

Foul Deeds and Suspicious Deaths in London's East End, Geoffrey Howse
ISBN: 1-903425-71-9. £10.99

Foul Deeds and Suspicious Deaths in Hampstead, Holborn & St Pancras,
Mark Aston
ISBN: 1-903425-94-8. £10.99

Foul Deeds and Suspicious Deaths in Hull, David Goodman
ISBN: 1-903425-43-3. £9.99

Foul Deeds and Suspicious Deaths Around Leicester, Kevin Turton
ISBN: 1-903425-75-1. £10.99

Foul Deeds and Suspicious Deaths in Manchester, Martin Baggoley
ISBN: 1-903425-65-4. £9.99

Foul Deeds and Suspicious Deaths in Newcastle, Maureen Anderson
ISBN: 1-903425-34-4. £9.99

Foul Deeds and Suspicious Deaths in Newport, Terry Underwood
ISBN: 1-903425-59-X. £9.99

Foul Deeds and Suspicious Deaths in and Around Scunthorpe, Stephen Wade
ISBN: 1-903425-88-3. £9.99

More Foul Deeds and Suspicious Deaths in Wakefield, Kate Taylor
ISBN: 1-903425-48-4. £9.99

Foul Deeds and Suspicious Deaths in York, Keith Henson
ISBN: 1-903425-33-6. £9.99

Foul Deeds and Suspicious Deaths on the Yorkshire Coast, Alan Whitworth
ISBN: 1-903425-01-8. £9.99

Please contact us via any of the methods below for more information or a catalogue.

WHARNCLIFFE BOOKS

47 Church Street – Barnsley – South Yorkshire – S70 2AS

Tel: 01226 734555 – 734222 Fax: 01226 734438

E-mail: enquiries@pen-and-sword.co.uk – Website: www.wharncliffebooks.co.uk

Foul Deeds & Suspicious Deaths Around

FOLKESTONE & DOVER

Martin Easdown and Linda Sage

Series Editor
Brian Elliott

Wharncliffe Books

First published in Great Britain in 2006 by
Wharncliffe Local History
an imprint of
Pen & Sword Books Ltd
47 Church Street
Barnsley
South Yorkshire
S70 2AS

ISBN 1 845630 11 4

Typeset in Plantin and Benguiat by
Phoenix Typesetting, Auldgirth, Dumfriesshire

Printed and bound in England by
CPI UK

Pen & Sword Books Ltd incorporates the Imprints of Pen
& Sword Aviation, Pen & Sword Maritime,
Pen & Sword Military, Wharncliffe Local History, Pen
and Sword Select, Pen and Sword Military Classics and
Leo Cooper.

For a complete list of Pen & Sword titles please contact
PEN & SWORD BOOKS LIMITED
47 Church Street
Barnsley
South Yorkshire
S70 2AS, England
E-mail: enquiries@pen-and-sword.co.uk
Website: www.pen-and-sword.co.uk

Contents

Acknowledgements

We would particularly like to thank for their assistance in this publication: Alan F. Taylor, Eamonn Rooney, Peter & Annie Bamford, Bob Hollingsbee, Roy & Jo Ingleton, Gary Cole, Brenda Howlett, John Calleja, Stella Boxall, Dover Discovery Centre, Folkestone Library, Hythe Library and the 2nd Infantry Brigade at Shorncliffe Camp.

Introduction

Murders provoke revulsion and fascination in all of us. The killing of a human being by another is an understandably emotive and controversial subject, but sadly one that has always been a part (if a totally abhorrent one) of the fabric of our lives. Yet each case can often tell us much about the area in which it took place and its inhabitants. This particularly applies to the poorer end of society, where the impoverished conditions were often a party to the crime committed.

Many of us may enjoy a good read about a classic old murder, but of course we are purely on the outside looking in. The thought that it may happen one day to one of our loved ones, for example, does not bear thinking about. A mercy killing, or even an act of self-defence, can perhaps be justified, but the murder of innocent children, in particular, is inexcusable and impossible to comprehend. To kill someone is the ultimate taboo; and that is why it scares us, but intrigues us too.

Foul Deeds and Suspicious Deaths Around Folkestone and Dover features a varied selection of dark acts committed in and around these famous Channel ports. The vulnerability of this stretch of coast facing the hostile intentions of Continental Europe led to the establishment of army bases in the area, yet the crowded and unsanitary conditions the soldiers had to put up with often led to violence. The military-related cases in this book feature a serviceman murdered in Dover because of his boots, the inexplicable killing of another by his best friend, and the strange death of a VC hero. The mysterious death of a Frenchman on the beach at Seabrook was said by some to have occurred because he was a suspected spy. During the Second World War Dover and Folkestone were nicknamed 'Hellfire Corner' due to the constant enemy action on the two towns. Sadly, death was not only meted out by the Germans, and included herein are the wartime murder of a cinema manager in Dover and the slaying of a young cinema usherette in an empty shop in Folkestone.

Although this corner of south-east Kent may not have been home to any particularly notorious crimes it was the scene of a couple of notable cases. The last woman to be publicly hanged in England was Frances Kidder, for killing her stepdaughter at New Romney, while the same year (1868) saw Thomas Wells become the first person to be privately hanged inside prison walls, for the murder of the stationmaster at Dover Priory station. The area also had its very own 'Jack the Ripper' scare in 1888, when a vagrant was held at the Elham Union workhouse on suspicion of being the Whitechapel Murderer!

Sadly, a number of the cases featured in this book involve the murder (or possible murder) of very young children by their mothers. Repugnant though these crimes were, there were often two main reasons why they were carried out: either to avoid the embarrassment and shame of having a child out of wedlock, or because the families were just too impoverished to support another little one. During a 32-year spell between 1890 and 1922 the regularity of newborn babies being left in parcels around Folkestone led to it being given the unenviable title of 'Infanticide Capital of Kent'. However, whether these were all cases of murder, or included some stillborn births, could not be definitely established, and anyway, little effort was made to catch the perpetrators.

A less extreme, but occasionally just as fatal, method of getting rid of unwanted children in Victorian times was to pay a 'Baby Farmer' to look after them. These women acted as foster mothers to the children, yet, in some cases, once the money was handed over the children were never seen again. We have included the possible murder of a Folkestone child by a Baby Farmer, along with the mysterious disappearance of servant girl Elizabeth Hearnden, which caused an almighty uproar in Folkestone in 1884.

It is a sad fact, however, that the younger members of our society are just as likely to suffer death at the hands of people that they know, particularly relatives. Poverty was often an underlying factor, as in the Hancock case of 1888 and the Dover Trunk Murder of 1936. The shame of a baby's father being revealed was another, as evident in the Wallace and Price cases. Yet, in the Kenward murder of 1908, which shocked middle-class Sandgate, Mrs Kenward took the reason for killing her daughter to her grave. That same year also saw William Bauldry murder his wife in the quiet village of Saltwood during an argument over their daughter's boots.

For the Bauldreys, the course of true love had ceased to run smoothly many years before, but crimes of passion and sexually motivated murder rear their ugly heads too. The oldest case in this book, the murder of John Lott in 1768, is the result of a classic *ménage à trois*, whilst the slaying of the Back sisters by Dedea Redanies in 1856 is probably the best-known, due to its immortalisation by a number of popular ballads of the time. At the other end of the scale is the little-known, but rather poignant, 'Hell hath no fury like a woman scorned' case from Folkestone's old fishing quarter. Bill Whiting was certainly one for the ladies in the 1930s, which led to him becoming embroiled in two murder cases in two years. In 1936 his estranged wife was killed by one of his acquaintances and then, two years later, Whiting himself was put on trial for murder, yet somehow managed to get himself acquitted.

Further stories of a murdered Dover policeman, a shooting on Folkestone's exclusive Leas Promenade and the 'House of Horror' complete our collection of stories from the darker side of Folkestone, Dover and their surrounding area. Each case has its own affecting points of interest, running the gamut of every human emotion, which hopefully may stir some of the reader's too.

CHAPTER 1

A Despicable Lott

Hythe and Burmarsh, 1768

A classic ménage à trois *crime in which all three participants meet a grisly end. A young servant girl marries her infatuated elderly employer on the urgings of her lover so she will inherit her husband's considerable wealth. To hasten his end they poison the old man, but the couple's actions easily arouse suspicion and the crime is soon discovered. They pay the ultimate price, but were they both equally responsible for carrying out the horrible deed?*

John Lott was a wealthy butcher and grazier who lived just off the High Street in Hythe. As well as holding grazing land in the area, he held considerable influence in the town and is known to have acted as a guarantor for the *White Hart*, *Sun* and *Duke's Head* public houses. In 1766 (the year he was fined 1s for 'throwing out dung and filth in the Back Lane', now Chapel Street/Prospect Road) Lott hired as a live-in maidservant an attractive young girl named Susannah. He soon became enamoured of her and offered the hand of marriage, but Susannah found him unattractive and kept refusing his proposals. The old man persisted, however, and in 1768 Susannah decided it would be best if she moved on.

The young maid went to live with her married sister at Rolvenden and there met Benjamin Buss, the brother of her sister's husband, Thomas Buss. She was instantly smitten with the handsome young man and they soon became close. On one occasion they stayed in London together for five days. Unfortunately, as Susannah was soon to discover, Benjamin Buss had a rather unsavoury side to his character and was involved in several dubious practices, including smuggling.

Lott, meanwhile, was not to be so easily deterred and called upon Susannah several times at Rolvenden urging her to marry him. Buss watched in amusement the old man's pleadings and hatched a plan. 'Why not marry him,' he asked Susannah, 'for upon his death you will inherit at least part of his substantial wealth?' Although the idea of marrying Lott still repulsed her,

The High Street, Hythe, in the area where John Lott lived. The old Smuggler's Retreat, with its look-out tower, was demolished in 1907. Marlinova Collection

Susannah eventually succumbed to Buss's urgings. Whether she knew of Buss's real intentions – to do away with Lott once the marriage had taken place – we do not know.

The marriage ceremony took place at Rolvenden on Monday, 15 August 1768 with Thomas Buss and his wife and Benjamin Buss in attendance. The wedding party then made their way to Lott's house in Hythe, where they stayed the night. Claiming he was unwell, Benjamin failed to return to Rolvenden with his brother and sister-in-law the following morning. However, the illness was almost certainly feigned and used as an excuse for Buss to stay on in Hythe and hatch the murder plan. He wasted no time in urging Susannah to poison her new husband and two days after the wedding showed her a packet he had obtained from Mr Gipps's apothecary that contained poison. He left it with her, although Susannah later claimed she threw it away.

After dinner on the following Wednesday, Lott took his wife and Buss on horseback to view some of his holdings. At Burmarsh they stopped for a pint of milk bumbo, which was a mixture of milk, rum, nutmeg and sugar. While Lott dismounted his horse to adjust the bridle, Buss was served the milk and passed it to Susannah to drink first. He then drank some before passing it onto Lott to finish off. Lott, however, complained that the drink had a 'very hot' taste and mentioned it to the woman innkeeper. She sampled the milk with her daughter and they found it had an unpleasant bitter taste. Upon throwing the rest of it away they noticed a sediment resembling paint on the bottom of the pot.

As they continued on their way, Buss confessed to Susannah he had slipped some of the poison into the milk before passing the drink over to Lott. Sure enough, the old man soon began to feel unwell and they stopped at Bonnington to drink tea. Buss made his cowardly excuses here and left to return to Rolvenden while Lott tried to get rid of the peppery taste in his mouth by drinking two dishes of tea, some brandy and water and a glass of gin. Not surprisingly, this made him feel even worse and on the journey back to Hythe he felt very ill and vomited several times. Lott's

The village of Burmarsh, where John Lott was poisoned with a pint of milk bumbo. Marlinova Collection

condition continued to worsen overnight and following a bout of violent sickness Susannah sent for an apothecary.

On the following morning (Thursday) Buss returned to Hythe and questioned Susannah on whether she had given her husband any more of the poison. On being told she had not and had thrown it away, he left the house and made his way to Folkestone. He returned during the afternoon with a bottle containing white powder, which was later identified as mercuric chloride, and told Susannah to give it to her husband. She later claimed she threw it into the privy, although her husband's condition remained poor over the weekend. Buss returned on Monday and it is probable he administered (with or without Susannah's knowledge and assistance) further doses of poison to John Lott. On Friday, 26 August 1768 Lott's body finally succumbed to the toxic onslaught and he died.

However, suspicions were quickly aroused over the sudden death of a man who had, until recently, been relatively strong and healthy. It had also not gone unnoticed that Lott's demise had coincided with his marriage to Susannah, whose friendship with Buss was commented upon.

The authorities were called in and soon traced the sale of poison to Buss at the Hythe apothecary. The ladies at the Burmarsh pub were also found and confirmed that they had felt ill after drinking the milk bumbo left by John Lott.

Susannah Lott was arrested and implicated Benjamin Buss in a statement taken at Hythe by William Deedes JP on 1 September 1768. The statement was not signed by Susannah but 'marked' and ends with the signature of Deedes under the attestation, 'Upon being confronted by Benjamin Buss, the person now in custody, she declared him to be the person of whom she had related the above circumstances.'

Susannah was imprisoned at Canterbury and was to remain there for seven months. She was then transferred to Maidstone to await her trial, but had to wait a further four months before that could begin. The delay was due to the illness of Mr Gipps, the Hythe apothecary, and in fact this important witness was to die before the trial commenced.

Early on in her internment Susannah was found to be pregnant and, due to the delay of the trial, gave birth in prison. Not surprisingly, she insisted the baby's father was John Lott, although many thought it more likely it was Benjamin Buss.

Upon his arrest, Buss claimed to be innocent of any charges and expressed his surprise that 'Mrs Lott should accuse him, who knew more of the matter than the magistrate who committed him.'

However, during his long period of imprisonment he signed a full confession after becoming convinced he was going to die of gaol fever. Buss's statement appeared to match Susannah's in almost every detail, but upon his recovery from the illness he retracted the confession.

The trial of Susannah Lott and Benjamin Buss finally commenced on 19 July 1769. Susannah's attitude was described as 'modest and penitent', whereas Buss was 'impudent and obdurate'. During the trial he maintained his innocence, claiming he had not visited the Lotts' house since the day of the wedding. However, two witnesses were produced who insisted he had stayed there the night before John Lott died. Buss's attempt to prove he had enjoyed no carnal relations with Susannah because he was married was also quickly disproved; despite his 'wife' swearing they had a contract of marriage.

Both were found guilty, with the court taking the view that Buss had taken up with Susannah in the hope of obtaining Lott's money. She had been an accessory to the crime, despite the pleas of innocence in her statement to Deedes. The fact that Lott stayed ill throughout the short-lived marriage, even between Buss's visits, probably proves that Susannah fed him at least some of the poison.

Upon hearing the verdict, Buss, who had behaved with insolent indifference throughout the trial, fell upon his knees and begged the court's mercy. He was sentenced to hang, with the body then being dissected and anatomised. Because her crime was classed as petty treason, Susannah was sentenced to be 'drawn upon a hurdle to the usual place of execution, and there to be burnt until she was dead.'

The sentences were carried out on 21 July 1769 at Penenden Heath, where executions had taken place for hundreds of years. From Maidstone Prison a wagon and four horses pulled Buss the two miles to the heath. Susannah, dressed in the black mourning clothes she had bought following her husband's death, followed on the hurdle, which was also drawn by four horses.

Buss was to meet his maker first. Upon the scaffold he made an apologetic last address begging forgiveness for his crime and acknowledging the justice of his sentence. He was then quickly despatched and his body left to hang for fifteen minutes. Buss's earlier plea not to be dissected after his death was respected and his body was buried instead.

Then it was Susannah's turn. Although her sentence called for her to be burned at the stake, by now it was usual practice to strangle or hang the convicted person first. So she was stood on a stool and fastened to a peg placed near the top of the seven-foot-high stake. The stool was then kicked away and like Buss she was left to hang for fifteen minutes, before being fastened with a chain to the stake. Bundles of faggots were placed around the base and set alight. A contemporary account records, 'she was soon reduced to ashes'.

CHAPTER 2

The Vanishing Murderer

Dover, 1844

This first, and very rare, murder of a Kent policeman in the course of his duty is noted for the total disappearance of the murderer. Although his identity was clearly established and his accomplices brought quickly to justice, Thomas Clark vanished into thin air and was never seen or heard of again.

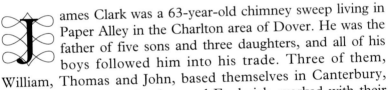 ames Clark was a 63-year-old chimney sweep living in Paper Alley in the Charlton area of Dover. He was the father of five sons and three daughters, and all of his boys followed him into his trade. Three of them, William, Thomas and John, based themselves in Canterbury, whilst the other two, Stephen and Frederick, worked with their father in Dover.

The Clarks were a rather rough and ready family who were known troublemakers. They liked nothing better than to go out drinking and instigating fights, particularly with members of the Beer family, with whom they had an ongoing feud.

On Sunday, 8 September 1844, a wet and windy day that would turn out to be stormy in more ways than one, all five Clark brothers were in Dover spending the afternoon in the *Admiral Harvey* public house. There they spotted the hated Beers and began taunting them. One of the brothers challenged Richard Beer to a fight for a sovereign, boasting he could 'kill' him within four rounds.

A full-scale brawl soon developed between the two families in the area around the pub, which attracted a large crowd. A policeman who lived in the vicinity, PC Pine, tried to calm the situation down and disperse the mob. However, as it grew in size he realised help was needed and sent his son off to the police station in Queen Street.

The Dover police force was hardly overmanned at this time, comprising of just a superintendent (in Folkestone that day), three sergeants and twelve constables. Nevertheless, a small band

The *Admiral Harvey* pub was a favoured hostelry for the troublesome Clark family. Marlinova Collection

of officers was gathered up and their arrival on the scene of the disturbance quickly led to the crowd's dispersal.

However, later that day, at around 9 p.m., the landlord of the *Admiral Harvey*, Fred Clements, reported that the Clarks were causing more trouble. The unruly family then moved on to the *Three Colts* beerhouse at the end of Paper Alley and were soon making life miserable for everyone in there. The landlady sent for the police, but upon their arrival the Clarks refused to leave the house. The head of the family, James Clark, was particularly vocal towards the police due to his drunken state and refused to budge an inch. PC Samuel Couchman called for assistance and met up with PC John Smith outside the *Royal Standard* pub in London Road. Together they went back to the *Three Colts*, but while Smith was attempting to arrest James Clark three men knocked him to the ground. Couchman, meanwhile, was trying to deal with the fights that had spilled out into the alley.

As PC Smith lay on the ground, Thomas Clark dragged his father into his cottage. He then came back out into the alley carrying a sweep's cane and brutally smashed it over the head of PC Couchman, who immediately slumped to the ground.

Witnessing the attack, Smith grappled with Clark, and deflecting a blow from the cane with his staff managed to wrest it from him. On hearing a cry of 'Murder!' the crowd quickly melted away.

A heavily bleeding Couchman was taken into Mr Flood's house in the alley and a surgeon was called for. Sadly, however, Couchman quickly succumbed to his injuries. The surgeon later told an inquest that death was due to a violent blow to the head with a blunt instrument, resulting in broken nasal bones that had caused severe bleeding and congestion of the brain.

Couchman, who had been in the Dover police force for two years following twenty-six years in the Royal Marines, left a wife and two children, who were provided for with a pension. He was laid to rest in St James's churchyard in front of the mayor and members of Dover Corporation.

Those who had witnessed the affray all pointed to Thomas Clark as the one who had struck the fatal blow, and the Clark family as the cause of the disturbance. James, Frederick and Stephen were quickly arrested, but William, Thomas and John, along with another wanted man named William Smith, had escaped.

A full-scale alert was put out for the wanted men and a £20 reward was offered for their capture. The three brothers were spotted in Chillenden Woods on the way to Canterbury, but had managed to escape before the superintendent and three constables from Dover Police could reach them. For nearly six weeks the brothers remained at large, until, in late October, William and John were traced living in a wood at Stockbury, close to the *Squirrels* pub. They had been inadvertently betrayed by their sister, who had told someone she was taking them food and clothes, which caused her to be followed. The brothers surrendered without a fight and after spending the night in Canterbury were taken to Dover.

Within a month William Smith was also apprehended and, along with James, William, John, Stephen and Frederick Clark, was tried for 'wilful murder and manslaughter' at Maidstone Assizes. However, because Thomas Clark, the real culprit, was still at large they were all acquitted of the charges.

Unfortunately, the troublesome Clarks were to remain a thorn in the side of law and order in Dover, and for some of them the chickens finally came home to roost. In 1846 Stephen was convicted of stealing a forty-pound cheese from a baker's shop in Priory Street and due to his bad record was sentenced to transportation for the remainder of his life. He had taken the opportunity to steal the cheese while both the proprietors were enjoying their supper beers in different pubs. Two years later Frederick carried out a robbery and rape and in 1853 he was sentenced to twenty years transportation. Another brother, William, was wrongly arrested and imprisoned in 1851 when he was mistaken for the missing Thomas!

However, the law was never to catch up with the elusive Thomas, the killer of PC Samuel Couchman. Nothing was seen or heard of him until 1853, when a man named Bishop reported he had seen him at the *Bell Inn*, Ivychurch, on the Romney Marsh. Bishop had worked as a sweep with Thomas in Canterbury and said he had also seen him some fifteen years previously at Ramsgate joining the crew of HMS *Boxer*. It was therefore surmised that Thomas had rejoined the navy after the murder, and this would explain his disappearance over the nine years since the murder.

A police officer was sent from New Romney to the pub and the suspect was placed in the town gaol for the night. Superintendent Coram of Dover Police was sent to fetch him the following day and they arrived back in Dover by train on 26 July in company

The *Bell Inn*, Ivychurch, where the man thought to be Thomas Clark was apprehended. Marlinova Collection

The murderer Thomas Clark was seen boarding HMS *Boxer* at Ramsgate Harbour. Marlinova Collection

with Alexander Williamson, the Chief Constable of Romney Marsh Police, and PC Geddes. News of the prisoner's return to Dover spread quickly and huge crowds lined the roads to the railway station.

Unfortunately, conflicting opinions soon emerged as to whether the prisoner was really Thomas Clark. PC Pine, who had attended the affray in Paper Alley involving Clark, thought it was him, yet most of the other witnesses disagreed. One of the Beer brothers who had fought with the Clarks during the day of the murder said the prisoner was definitely not Thomas Clark. A Mr Portwine agreed: he had known Thomas since he was a boy and the prisoner looked nothing like him. For a start he was nearly six foot tall, whereas Thomas was only five foot six, and furthermore his voice was totally different. In addition, Clark had a mermaid and a woman with a ring pricked on his arm, but when the prisoner bared his arms there were no marks visible.

Nevertheless, the prisoner was adjourned to court, where his twin brother verified with a birth certificate that he was in fact John Merritt. Four other witnesses also testified that he was definitely not Thomas Clark. The authorities, much to the disappointment of the Dover townsfolk, let the prisoner go into the care of his brother, who had a job lined up for him in London.

The real Thomas Clark was never seen or heard of again. We know Bishop was totally mistaken in identifying Clark at Ivychurch, so perhaps he never saw him boarding HMS *Boxer* at Ramsgate either. However, it does seem feasible that to escape justice Clark did rejoin the Royal Navy under an assumed name and sailed off into the sunset to start a new life.

CHAPTER 3

An Unrequited Love

Capel-le-Ferne/Folkestone, 1856

A famous case, commemorated in verse and ballad, involving two sisters who were murdered by the jealous fiancé soldier of one of them.

Caroline and Maria Back were the Belles of the Ball amongst the young men of Dover. The two pretty sisters, aged 18 and 16 respectively, were never short of admirers, particularly amongst the military stationed in the town. They lived with their parents, John and Mary, at 3 Albion Place, Dover, and Caroline assisted her mother in running a small laundry business. Amongst the clothes they handled were the uniforms of local soldiers, whose eyes would invariably light

Albion Place, where the Back sisters lived. Bob Hollingsbee

up when greeted by one of the pretty sisters. Usually this would be Caroline, as Maria also worked as a servant at Kington confectioners in Snargate Street.

One evening, the two sisters were at the theatre when they were noticed by a swarthy 26-year-old Serbian soldier named Dedea Redanies. He was based with the 4th Company of the 2nd Battalion in the 2nd Regiment British Swiss Legion, although before coming to Britain he had already led a colourful life.

The son of a Moslem civil servant at a time when Serbia was under Turkish rule, Redanies joined a cavalry regiment of the Austro-Hungarian army. An undoubtedly brave soldier, he had suffered capture and wounding, and on one occasion was awarded a gold medal after capturing the enemy's colours disguised as a seller of spirits. Redanies also saw service with the Austrians in Italy and later switched sides and joined the Italian army! While in Milan, he was baptised as a Christian by a Serbian Capuchin monk. However, upon hearing of the formation of the British Foreign Legions, he deserted the Italians and made his way to Switzerland, where he enlisted with the British Swiss Legion.

Upon reaching England, Redanies' ability to speak German and Italian landed him a job as an interpreter with the military hospital at Dover Castle. After meeting the Back girls at the theatre he became a regular visitor to their house, initially accompanied by a bundle of laundry. However, he soon fell in love with Caroline and within a short time her family was regarding him as her fiancé.

Unfortunately, Redanies soon revealed he was possessed of a somewhat jealous streak. During one evening visit to the house, he bumped into an artilleryman coming down the stairs. He became agitated as to why the man was there, but later appeared to forget about it after he had spent some time with Caroline.

Shortly after this incident, Redanies was posted to Aldershot for a few months, and while he was away he wrote several letters to his intended and her family. Alas, for the unfortunate lovestruck Serbian, Caroline's affections towards him had noticeably cooled during his absence, and her attentions wandered off elsewhere. This was brought home to Redanies on his return to Dover when he asked Caroline to show him the letters he had written to her while he was away. She mistakenly handed him a letter from another admirer before realising her error and snatching it back. Yet Redanies had seen enough of the letter to notice the lines 'My Dear Caroline' and 'looking forward to meeting you again in Woolwich'.

For the time being Redanies managed to keep his emotions

under control, but on Saturday, 2 August 1856 matters reached a head. Caroline announced to Redanies that she was going to stay with her married sister, Mary, in Woolwich. The soldier, remembering the snatched letter with the reference to meeting someone in Woolwich, exploded with jealousy. He accused Caroline of flirting with a sergeant at Shorncliffe Camp (whom she had never actually met) before demanding back the small portrait of him he had given her. When she gave it to him he responded by smashing the frame against a hearth and throwing the photograph in the fire.

Redanies remained agitated throughout the afternoon and at around 6 p.m. he went to John Green's cutlers shop in Snargate Street and purchased a poniard, a type of small dagger. By 7.30 p.m. he had returned to the Back house and asked Caroline to accompany him early the next morning to Folkestone. Mary Back was firmly against the idea because Caroline had not been feeling well and a doctor had advised her to rest; yet Redanies was most insistent that the walk would do her good. Reluctantly Mrs Back agreed, on the condition Maria would accompany them as a chaperone.

Where Redanies spent the remainder of that evening is unclear. The Back house is the likely place, although John and Mary Back later vehemently denied this. John Back stated that he arose at 3 a.m. on the Sunday morning and had breakfast with his daughters and Redanies (who was wearing his uniform red jacket and cap) before they set off for Folkestone at around 3.30 a.m. An hour-and-a-half later, Redanies was spotted walking arm-in-arm with the sisters outside the *Royal Oak* public house near Capel-le-Ferne.

What happened next is from the account Redanies gave to the police after his arrest. He told them he had taken the girls off the road to sit down and rest on the grass, but they refused, saying the grass was too damp. He then asked Caroline if she would walk on ahead and as she did so he moved around behind Maria and plunged a knife directly into her heart. A muffled cry managed to pass her lips before she slumped to the ground dead from stab wounds. Seeing what happened, Caroline fell to her knees crying, where she was kissed and embraced by Redanies. The terrified woman frantically tried to grab the knife, in the process cutting her hands, but her fiancé proceeded to plunge the weapon three times fatally into her chest. The murderer then took the black capes the girls had been wearing and left the scene of the crime, weeping.

For around two hours the lifeless bodies of the Back sisters lay

The *Valiant Sailor* pub, situated just inside the Folkestone boundary. It was at the back of the inn that the murder of the Back sisters by Dedea Redanies took place. Marlinova Collection

on the cliff-top at Steddy Hole, above Folkestone Warren, where they were discovered by a Folkestone carpenter named Thomas Girling. He ran to the nearby *Valiant Sailor* inn to inform the landlord, Richard Kitham, of his grisly finds. The police were

A view looking towards Dover and the famous white cliffs from the site of the Back sisters' slaying at Steddy Hole. Marlinova Collection

Looking in the other direction from the murder site, we see the town of Folkestone below. Marlinova Collection

called and they summoned surgeon William Bateman to examine the bodies. He concluded that both girls had been stabbed in the chest a number of times, causing instantaneous death. The bodies were then taken to a nearby house, where Mary Back later positively identified them.

Meanwhile, Redanies was making his way towards Canterbury. He was seen at around 6 a.m. at Black Robin's Camp, Barham Downs, then at Broome Park, where he was given some bread and cheese. At Lower Hardres he stopped at Mrs Elizabeth Attwood's grocers shop to buy writing paper, envelopes and a pen. He then wrote two letters in German confessing the crime, one to his commanding officer, Lieutenant Wilhelm Schmidt, and the following to Mary Back (translated into English):

Dearest Mother Back – On the first lines I pray to forgive the awful occurrence to the unlucky Dedea Redanies which I committed on my dear Caroline and Maria Back yesterday morning; at five o'clock I perpetrated the horrible deed. Scarcely I am able to write by heart-break for my ever-memorable Caroline and Maria. The cause of this deed is – 1. I heard that Caroline is not in the family way, as I first believed – 2. Because Caroline intends to go to Woolwich – 3. That I cannot stay with my very dear Caroline it made my heart so confused till at last the unhappy thought came into my head that Caroline rather may die from my hands, than to allow Caroline's love being bestowed upon another.

However I did not intend to murder also Maria her sister; but not having another opportunity and as she was in my way I could not do otherwise than stab her too.

Dear Mother Back – Saturday evening when I came I had not the least trace of this awful act. But as I learned that my dear Caroline gave me back my likeness and as she told me she would leave I did not know any other way in my heartbreak than go to the Cutlers and I brought a poniard which divided the hearty lovers.

Arm in arm I brought both my dearest souls in the world over to the unlucky place near the road before Folkestone and requested them to sit down. But the grass being wet they refused to do so and I directed then Caroline to go forward and I went behind Maria into whose heart I run the dagger. With a dull cry she sank down. With a most broken heart I rushed then after Caroline, lifting the poniard in my hands towards her. Dear Dedea cried she with a half dead voice and fell down with weeping eyes. Then I rushed over her and gave her the last kisses as an everlasting remembrance.

I could not live a more dreadful hour in my life than that was; and from my broken heart I knew not where my senses were, and I took as a lasting keepsake both the black shawls of Maria and my dear Caroline as a mourning suit for me leaving the awful spot with weeping eyes and a broken heart.

Never I shall forget my dear Caroline and Maria and the poniard remains covered with the blood of Maria and Caroline with me until it will pierce my own breast and I shall see my dear Maria and Caroline in the eternal life.

Farewell and be not troubled about the blissfully deceased angels of God and forgive the unhappy ever weeping.
Dedea Redanies
3 August 1856

Upon finishing the letters, he went to the village post office, bought two stamps and put them in the letterbox.

Redanies then continued on towards Canterbury, but on the Ashford turnpike road at Chartham he was spotted by PC George Fryer of Thannington still wearing the Back sisters' shawls. As

Fryer approached him Redanies proceeded to stab himself several times but nevertheless he was arrested and taken to Dover police station. During an examination the seriousness of his wounds was discovered and he was taken to hospital for treatment. The location of the two letters was also revealed and Police Superintendent William Walker was sent to the letterbox at Lower Hardres with a magistrate's order for their appropriation.

Once his wounds had been treated, Redanies was kept at Folkestone Gaol until he was sent for trial at Maidstone Assizes in December 1856. He pleaded guilty to murdering Caroline (but not Maria); although his defence argued that he was not of sound mind when the acts were committed, as evident by the rambling letters and his wandering around the countryside wearing the Back sisters' shawls. Nevertheless, it took the jury only two minutes to convict him.

Donning the black cap, the judge concluded:

Your offence is not as hateful as though it had proceeded from the motive of obtaining the property of another; or by revenge; or any other motive hateful or detestable in itself. But you have allowed an ill-regulated passion to get the mastery over you and your conduct is, in reality, as selfish and as wicked as if it proceeded from any of the motives I have mentioned. Although, therefore, one may pity you more, it is necessary to make an example as much in this as in any case of murder.

Redanies appeared unmoved by the sentence of death and walked calmly from the dock. While awaiting his execution, he requested a meeting with the Backs, and Mary travelled up to see him. He greeted her warmly and asked for forgiveness, which she gave.

An unsuccessful effort to halt the death sentence because of the prisoner's sanity was made by a Roman Catholic priest, Father Lawrence. Redanies handed the priest a letter to be given to the Backs after his execution. It read:

Dear parents, forget your anger against me and do not curse me in my grave. Remember that by doing so you would not only afflict me but also my dear Caroline and Maria. They love me as I love them. We are above with our father again together, where we shall see one another again and live forever with the father of love, Jesus Christ.

I greet you, with my dear Caroline and Maria, and wish you the blessings of God and prosperity until the voice of God calls you, too, to life everlasting.
Caroline Back, Dedea Redanies, Maria Back

Following a restless night, Redanies arose early on New Year's Day 1857 and attended a service in the prison chapel at 8.45. He then returned to his cell before being fetched for his execution by Calcraft, the executioner. He was pinioned and led out to the scaffold, which had been erected on the porter's lodge. A crowd of around four or five thousand had gathered to watch the drama, some of whom heard Redanies utter his final words, 'In a few moments I will be in the arms of my dear Caroline. I do not care about my death.'

A sad sequel to the execution occurred while the temporary gallows were being dismantled. James Anderson, one of the two men engaged on the task, unfortunately lost his balance and fell to his death.

The public's fascination with the Redanies case resulted in a number of ballads being written about it. Two of them, *The Life, Trial and Execution of Dedea Redanies for the Murder of Caroline and Maria Back* and *The Dying Soldier at Maidstone Gaol*, both printed by J. Powell, are now largely forgotten. However, the third ballad, *The Folkestone Murder*, printed by Henry Disley of Seven Dials, found its way into popular culture. The full version reads:

> *Kind friends come pay attention, and listen to my song,*
> *It is about a murder and it won't detain you long,*
> *'Twas near the town of Folkestone this shocking deed was*
>   *done,*
> *Maria and sweet Caroline were murder'd by Switzerland*
>   *John.*
>
> *He came unto their parents' house at nine o'clock one night,*
> *But little did poor Caroline think he ow'd her any spite;*
> *'Will you walk me with, dear Caroline?' the murderer did*
>   *say,*
> *And she agreed to accompany him to Shorncliffe Camp the*
>   *next day.*
>
> *Said the mother to the daughter, 'You'd better stay at home;*
> *It is not fit for you to go with that young man alone;*
> *You'd better take your sister to go along with you,*
> *Then I have no objection, dear daughter, you may go.'*
>
> *Early next morning, before the break of day,*
> *Maria and sweet Caroline from Dover Town did stray,*
> *But before they reach'd Folkestone the villain drew a knife;*
> *Maria and sweet Caroline he robb'd them of their lives.*

*Down on their knees the sisters fell, all in their blooming
      years;*
*'For mercy' cried, 'We're innocent', their eyes were fill'd with
      tears;*
*He plung'd the knife into their breasts, their lovely breasts so
      deep;*
*He robb'd them of their own sweet lives and left them there to
      sleep.*

*Three times he kiss'd their cold pale lips as they lay on the
      ground,*
*He took the capes for off their backs, for on him they were
      found;*
*He said, 'Farewell sweet Caroline, your blood my hands has
      stain'd;*
*No more on earth shall I see you but in heaven we will meet
      again.'*

Early next morning their bodies were found,
*At a lonely place call'd Steady Hall, a-bleeding on the
      ground;*
And if you ever go unto the spot, these letters you will find,
Cut deep in the grass so green: Maria and Caroline.

*When the news it reach'd their parents' ears, they cried
      'What shall we do?*
Maria has been murder'd, and lovely Caroline too.'
*They pull'd and tore their old grey hair, in sorrow and in
      shame,*
And tears they roll'd in torrents from their poor aged cheeks.

This murderer has been taken, his companions to him deny,
And he is sent to Maidstone and is condemn'd to die;
*He said 'Farewell' to all his friends, 'In this world I am
      alone,*
And have to die for murder far from my native land.'

'The dismal bell is tolling, the scaffold I must prepare,
*I trust in heaven my soul shall rest and meet sweet Caroline
      there;*
Now all young men take warning from this sad fate of mine,
To the memory of Maria Back and sweet Caroline.'

CHAPTER 4

The Missing Boots

Dover, 1856

If there was ever an open-and-shut case this was it. A soldier shoots a colleague in cold blood in front of a number of witnesses; and within three hours he is up before the Magistrates' Court. The Guilty verdict and his subsequent execution were a foregone conclusion; thus the lives of two young men were thrown away, all for a pair of boots.

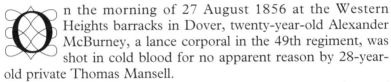

n the morning of 27 August 1856 at the Western Heights barracks in Dover, twenty-year-old Alexander McBurney, a lance corporal in the 49th regiment, was shot in cold blood for no apparent reason by 28-year-old private Thomas Mansell.

The act was committed at around 8.30 a.m. in front of several witnesses. One of them, John Parry, a private in the 49th regiment, remembered:

At half past eight o'clock this morning, as I came out of my tent at the camp in the Hospital Meadow, I passed between the prisoner and the deceased; and in passing, I felt that something touched my arm, upon which I looked round, when I saw the prisoner, with his firelock close against the right side of the deceased. I then heard a report from the prisoner's firelock, and McBurney cried out 'I am shot.' The deceased cried out two or three times that he was shot, and the last time he cried out that Mansell had shot him. The prisoner then threw down the firelock, and said 'Now then.' He then walked away a distance of seven or eight yards, and I followed him and took hold of him. He was afterwards ordered to the guardhouse, where I saw him removed by two other soldiers. The deceased was on his knees at the time he was shot, cleaning his things, but then arose, and staggered back a few paces, and dropped. I took up the firelock with which the prisoner shot the deceased, and gave it into the custody of the Superintendent of Police, Mr Coram. That produced is the same. It is an Enfield rifle. The rifle was not loaded in consequence of any duty the prisoner had had to perform; he had no business to have any ammunition at all. The gun cap was on the nipple, and had exploded.

The incident was also described by another private in the regiment, Edward Brophey:

This morning about half-past eight, immediately after my breakfast, I was coming out of my tent, when I saw the prisoner with his fire-lock in his hand, which I thought he was going to clean. I saw him cock the piece, and saw a cap on it. I supposed he was going to snap the cap, to clear the piece, as is frequently done. The deceased was then kneeling [this was denied by Mansell, who said McBurney was standing] about six yards from the prisoner, who, as I have said, appeared to be going to snap off the cap. At this instant, the witness Parry came out of his tent, and passed between the prisoner and the deceased, while Mansell approached close to McBurney, and shot him. The deceased put his hand to his right side, and exclaimed 'I am shot, Mansell has shot me.' Mansell threw down his rifle after firing, and walked away five or six yards, but then appeared to hear what the deceased said, as the prisoner turned round when McBurney said Mansell had shot him, and both their

The Western Heights Barracks, Dover, where Lance Corporal Alexander McBurney was killed because of his boots. Bob Hollingsbee

The military hospital, where Alexander McBurney died. Marlinova Collection

faces met. The deceased was afterwards removed to the Military Hospital and I saw his body there: the shot appeared to have entered his right side and passed out at his left, as the elbow was injured.

Peter Moran also saw the shooting and found the rifle ball:

I was one of the escort who took Mansell to the guard room. On my return there was a large crowd around the deceased, who was then dying from the wound he had received. Towards the evening there was a crowd of soldiers and civilians looking for the ball on the earth. I saw where it had entered, and got a spade and dug it up. That produced is the same: it is an Enfield rifle ball, and such as were served to us in the Crimea, and would fit the firelock produced. Mansell was not a communicative man.

Indeed, Mansell, who had served for ten years in the regiment, was described as being 'reserved and of bad temper: if offended he would not speak to the offending party for years'. He had fought with honour in the Crimean campaign and gained a Good Conduct medal.

McBurney was more popular with his colleagues. He came from the north of Ireland and had enlisted in February 1854. However, he had been ill for most of the time the regiment had been stationed in Dover and was discharged from hospital just a few days before he was killed. He was laid to rest at Copt Hill cemetery.

At Dover police station PC Thomas Back heard Mansell's reasons for the killing:

> *He said it is done, I am sorry for that, I had no intention to do it when I got up this morning. He then said that a new pair of boots had been served out to him at the Crimea, which he did not want at the time. They were sent to England in a squad bag, and when the bag was opened, his new boots were gone, and an old pair, belonging to McBurney, were found in their place. He complained to the commanding officer, but could get no redress and he had lost nine shillings by it. He thought McBurney was allowed to rob the soldiers with impunity and he always thought he was right.*

Mansell clearly had harboured a grudge against McBurney, although according to John Parry there seemed to be no particular animosity between them:

> *I was in the same tent with Mansell and McBurney when in the Crimea; and they slept side by side. In the Hospital Meadow, the deceased's tent was next to mine; but I don't know where Mansell's was, of my own knowledge I know of nothing unpleasant that existed between them, but I have heard of some dispute about a pair of boots. Mansell is a man of sullen disposition, and he but seldom conversed with his comrades. Sometimes he would pass three or four weeks without speaking, unless spoken to.*

Private Benjamin Taylor was a witness to Mansell's simmering resentment over the boots:

> *Thomas Mansell has lived under the same tent as myself since throughout the regiment being quartered at Dover. One night last week, about a week ago, Mansell and I were in the tent alone, when he told me 'I suppose you know about those boots of mine that were lost.' I answered 'No; I know nothing about them.' He then said, 'I am sure McBurney knows something about it; and I will have it in for him, if I live for a thousand years.' I don't know what he meant by the words 'I will have it in for him' but I understood it as a threat. The deceased had been in hospital up to within four or five*

days of his being shot, Mansell lost his boots in the Crimea. I don't know the facts of the dispute touching the boots. Mansell had never spoken to me about McBurney before.

At the coroner's inquest Mansell was found guilty of murder. While he was being held in prison awaiting trial he appeared to show some remorse for his crime when he burst into tears during an interview with the prison governor. Further repentance was shown in a letter he wrote to a colleague in his regiment, although he also justified why he carried out the shooting:

My dear friend – I write to you these few lines hoping they will, by the blessing of God, find you in good health, as it leaves me at present. Thank God for it. My dear friend James, the reason I take the liberty of writing to you is, to know what you think of my ease. I myself might differ in opinion to other people; but I do not differ in what it really was, or, as far as I am sure, it was a case of great excitement and irritation. I could plainly see the man was deter-mined to get me into trouble one day or the other. I cannot say positively that he done it, but he claimed the boots as soon as ever I took them out of my bag...no doubt expecting when he saw me go into my bag, that I should have taken the bag into my tent; and if I had done so, no doubt his intention was to follow me and search my bag, well knowing his boots would be found there, and, of course, he would have had me confined. I am extremely sorry for the crime I have committed, but I could not avoid it, for I was worked up that fatal morning to a pitch of madness, and I hardly knew what I had done. My dear friend – I am as comfortable as can be expected, considering the place I am in, and what I am in for. Please let me know if my boots was found in the deceased's things afterwards, and please let me know all the particulars. Please write to me as soon as you possibly can for I long to hear from you. Please let me know what public opinion is. Please give my best respects to drummer Money, and all inquiring friends, and reserve the same yourself – so no more at present from your truly friend Thomas Mansell.

Mansell pleaded not guilty at his trial at Maidstone Assizes, but the verdict was a foregone conclusion. The jury (whose members had been challenged by both the prosecution and defence coun-sels) quickly found the prisoner guilty and he was sentenced to death. It was not revealed whether indeed Mansell's boots were found in the dead man's possession.

CHAPTER 5

The Guilty Secret

Dover, 1856

From the lips of the few who had seen the harrowing spectacle, of the little innocent bathed in blood, with her head nearly severed from her body, on the hearth that barely an hour before had witnessed her guileless smiles, the dreadful intelligence of what transpired was rapidly circulated through the town; and its effect was to create a sensation probably unequalled in intensity by any circumstances within the memory of the oldest resident.

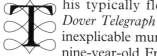his typically florid and sensational account in the *Dover Telegraph* hid what was basically a very sad and inexplicable murder of a child by her mother. Twenty-nine-year-old Frances Wallace, known as Fanny, lived in a small cottage at 15 Town Wall Lane, Dover, having returned to live in the town from London some three years previously. She was the daughter of the former manager of the *Ship Hotel* and when young was looked after by Mrs Mary Westow in Woolcomber Lane. Now Mrs Westow looked after Fanny's own five-year-old daughter, also known as Frances, when she was working as a laundress.

Fanny was by all accounts a very good mother, but was shameful of the fact she was not married to the child's father. However, this had never been on the cards due to the fact her daughter's father was her brother-in-law! Fanny had kept this guilty secret to herself for the past five years, but unfortunately had recently let it slip to a Scotsman named Bligh with whom she had become friendly. Bligh, who lived next-door and was employed at the Admiralty Yard, duly passed on the secret to his landlord, Mr Wells, who told him it was only right that Fanny's sister should be told of the truth.

Bligh told Fanny what Wells had said and then insinuated that he would be travelling on the six o'clock train up to London the next morning to reveal all to her sister. Fanny became ill with worry and was convinced she was going to die. She appears anyway to have been something of a hypochondriac and was

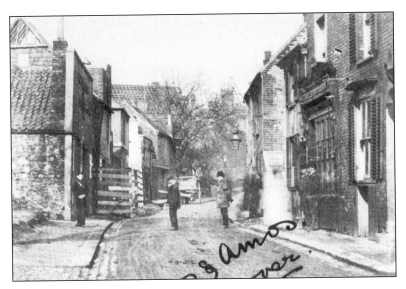

Child-killer Fanny Wallace was brought up in Woolcomber Lane, Dover. Dover Museum

prone to bouts of mental instability. Fanny spent that evening comforting her daughter, who could not sleep, before undergoing a restless night herself.

On the following morning, Sunday, 26 October 1856, Fanny arose at five with her mind still in turmoil over the imminent departure of the six o'clock train and its deliverer of her guilty secret. Some two hours later, shortly after seven, loud screams were heard coming from her cottage. The neighbours who rushed to the scene found Fanny sobbing and trembling uncontrollably. One of her hands was covered with blood and when asked what had happened she told them, 'I have been and murdered my own child – go in and look.'

Elizabeth Mitchell, who lived at 1 Town Wall Lane, entered the house and found the child's body by the fireplace covered in blood. Upon closer examination she found that the throat had almost been cut through and the head was close to being severed from the body. Lying nearby in a pool of blood was the weapon used to carry out the horrible deed, a case knife. When asked why she had killed her daughter, Fanny told them it was because Bligh was going to reveal her secret to her sister.

While Elizabeth Mitchell went off to fetch the police her husband John stayed with Fanny. When he asked her why she had done it, all she could say was, 'That man'.

PC Thomas Irons was sent back with Mrs Mitchell to Fanny's cottage. He found her to be delirious: her arms and hands were covered in blood and she kept repeating 'Oh policeman, what a hardened wretch I am and that innocent dear, that innocent creature.' She also kept referring to the London train, asking repeatedly, 'Does it go at six?' When Irons expressed ignorance of the times, she told him, 'If that man's gone to my sister's, there will be murder upon murder – there will be double murder.'

After examining the knife (which he thought to have been recently sharpened) Irons took Fanny into custody. At the station she asked the police to telegram her sister's husband so he could leave for Dover before Bligh reached London. During questioning she told them there was a sugar of lead at home. This was a poison that perhaps she had intended to take herself or to feed to her daughter. After being questioned, Fanny was charged with the murder of her daughter.

On the following day, she appeared at the magistrates' court at the Maison Dieu, where she cut a very pitiful figure. Looking very sick and haggard, Fanny fainted before the proceedings had even started and was sat on a chair. Upon being told she was charged

Fanny Wallace was hauled up before the Magistrates' Court at the Maison Dieu on the charge of killing her young daughter. Bob Hollingsbee

with wilful murder she asked for time to think, before replying, 'I have nothing to say'.

Throughout the hearing Fanny was beside herself with grief, particularly whenever the child was mentioned, which solicited a good deal of sympathy for her from those in court. It was even claimed the magistrates, who included the Mayor of Dover, were moved to tears! Nevertheless, the Mayor had the sad duty to inform the prisoner that she would be committed for trial at Maidstone Assizes.

Fanny was taken to Maidstone Gaol to await her trial, which would take place in December. Meanwhile, an inquest into the death of the child also recorded a Guilty verdict against Fanny. The body of her deceased daughter was removed to the residence of Mrs Westow before it was laid to rest in Copt Hill Cemetery on Friday, 31 October.

At her trial, Fanny still looked very poorly and once again remained seated throughout. Elizabeth Mitchell and PC Irons both gave evidence and Irons produced the murder knife, which was still covered in blood. All of the witnesses spoke of Fanny's affection for her daughter, including an old woman named Charlotte Barton, who lodged with her. She revealed that the child only stayed with her mother at weekends, and on the Saturday night before her murder Fanny had retired to bed about 9.30 after the child had fallen asleep. She awoke early the next morning and complained to Mrs Barton she was restless because of the old lady's coughing. Barton had seen Bligh at the house on a couple of occasions, but did not think he was particularly intimate with Fanny.

Fanny was obviously guilty of the crime, but was she also of sound mind when she committed it? The police themselves admitted that her behaviour in custody was 'frantic', and the defence played the insanity card by highlighting the lack of a real motive, the mother's affection for her child and her incomprehensible behaviour. They further argued that if Fanny's mind was normal she would have used the poison on the child and concealed the murder.

The jury was swayed by the defence's arguments and a returned a Not Guilty verdict on the grounds of insanity. Fanny was ordered to be detained indefinitely at Her Majesty's pleasure.

CHAPTER 6

The Secretive Frenchman

Seabrook, 1866

This was a mystifying case all round, and the sensation of 1866 in Folkestone and Sandgate. An enigmatic Frenchman, at pains not to reveal his identity and keen to visit Shorncliffe army camp, is found dead on Seabrook beach. The coroner's verdict of suicide causes a howl of protest, as it clearly seems this was a case of robbery and murder. Yet, if the secretive Frenchman was a spy, were darker forces at play?

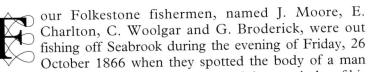

Four Folkestone fishermen, named J. Moore, E. Charlton, C. Woolgar and G. Broderick, were out fishing off Seabrook during the evening of Friday, 26 October 1866 when they spotted the body of a man face-down with his head just in the water and the remainder of his body lying on the beach. A closer examination revealed him to be dead, and a number of bruises could clearly be seen on his head, causing the fishermen to alert both the coastguard at Sandgate and the police at Seabrook.

A search of the dead man's clothes revealed a silver pocket-watch with a platinum chain and a large amount of both British and French currency, along with a timetable and a letter written in French. It was therefore deduced that the deceased was a wealthy Frenchman of about forty years of age.

Further enquires established that this was the same Frenchman who had stayed at the *Alexandra Hotel*, Folkestone during the previous night. However, the manager of the hotel, Charles Spurrier, was unable to supply a definite name for his guest, who appeared reluctant to give one. During his stay the Frenchman had expressed a wish to visit Shorncliffe Camp and was shown by Mr Spurrier the directions to take. He was expected back at the hotel later that day, but failed to arrive.

The next clear-cut sighting of the deceased was at around 9 p.m. on the evening of his death, when he was seen in the company of two prostitutes and an officer's servant in Mr Wickes's beershop, the *Sebastopol*, in Sandgate. The party then

The *Alexandra Hotel*, Folkestone, where the mysterious Frenchman took lodgings and asked the landlord the way to Shorncliffe Camp.
Eamonn Rooney

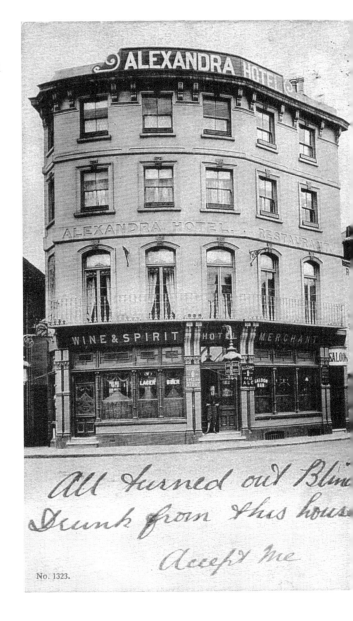

moved on to the Alhambra Theatre, yet all efforts thereafter to establish a sighting of the deceased between the time he left the theatre and the finding of his body on the beach at 10.30 p.m. were unsuccessful. A gang of workmen had been working on the beach up to 9.40 p.m. and they saw or heard nothing, which meant that the crime (or suicide) had occurred between 9.40 and

10.30. Furthermore, the incident would have taken place in full view of any passers-by on the busy Sandgate–Hythe road, yet no one saw anything.

Against all expectations, the coroner decided on a verdict of suicide, yet that was rightly criticised as being 'the usual refuge in doubtful cases'. The blows on the temple alone make suicide seem unlikely, but in addition, the idea of the deceased standing a yard from the sea and throwing himself face-forward into what amounted to an inch of water in an attempt at self-drowning seems absurd.

However, those in favour of the Suicide verdict pointed out the large amount of valuables that were left on the body. Yet it was known that the deceased had been wearing a bag of money suspended around his neck while in Sandgate, and this had gone missing. The other valuables appeared to have been ignored, because either the main booty had been secured, they were simply not found, or the robbers had been disturbed in their work.

The logical conclusion to the case is that the deceased was robbed and murdered by persons unknown (perhaps the prostitutes and officer's servant) for his purse of money: either on the beach or at a spot somewhere in Sandgate before he was dumped on the beach at Seabrook.

Sandgate High Street, with the Alhambra Music Hall pictured on the far right. This was where the mysterious Frenchman was last seen. *Marlinova Collection*

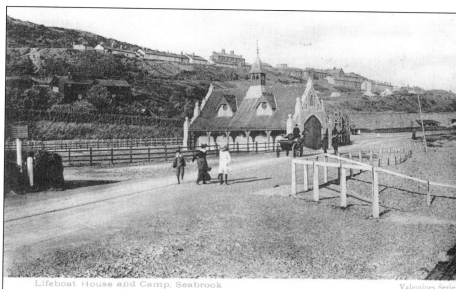

The beach at Seabrook where the body of the Frenchman was found. The old lifeboat station (nicknamed the 'Goose Cathedral' by Jocelyn Brooke) can be seen, and up on the hill is Shorncliffe Camp. Marlinova Collection

The claim that the deceased was murdered because he was a spy can be discounted. His willingness to visit Shorncliffe Camp was probably harmless, although ill-advised in those days of often-hostile Anglo-French relations.

The identity of the mysterious Frenchman was eventually traced through a handkerchief found on his body containing the initials 'O.L.' He was found to be Monsieur Lavernelle, who was then laid to rest in St Martin's Church, Cheriton on 30 October 1866.

However, on 22 June 1867 the *Folkestone Observer* recorded:

> *The body of the French gentleman who was probably murdered sometime ago at Seabrook has this week been exhumed, and removed to France, in which country he was an Inspector of Telegraphs.*

What the newspaper neglected to say, however, was that six coffins were dug up before they found the right one! The secretive Frenchman had proved elusive right to the end.

CHAPTER 7

Fit for the Last Drop

New Romney, 1867

The vicious and unforgivable atrocity of Frances Kidder murdering her young stepdaughter has gone down in the annals of crime as the last public hanging of a woman in England. For, just a month following Kidder's execution on 28 April 1868, the passing of the Capital Punishment Within Prisons Bill on 29 May 1868 abolished public executions in Britain. Just three days earlier, Michael Barrett, a Fenian, had been the last person to suffer a public execution.

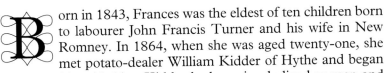 orn in 1843, Frances was the eldest of ten children born to labourer John Francis Turner and his wife in New Romney. In 1864, when she was aged twenty-one, she met potato-dealer William Kidder of Hythe and began a relationship with him. Kidder had previously lived as man and wife (although they were not married) with a woman named Staples, who bore him two children but had recently died. Frances herself quickly became pregnant by Kidder and they were married in 1865 shortly after the child was born. They established a home in Hythe, which housed Kidder, Frances, their baby and Kidder's two children.

Unfortunately, Frances took an instant dislike to her husband's children by Staples. The younger child was quickly packed off to live with relatives, but the eldest, Louisa, stayed with her father and new stepmother. Born in 1856, Louisa was nine years old, but looked younger: she was apparently cross-eyed, yet possessed a sunny, exuberant nature. Sadly that was soon to be knocked out of her by the malicious Frances, who regularly enjoyed beating her with a broomstick. In addition, the child was starved, dressed in rags and made to sleep on empty potato sacks in the cellar.

Why Frances Kidder had such a pathological hatred of the child is unclear. Perhaps it was just plain jealousy. Her husband initially did little to stop the abuse, but the next-door neighbour, carpenter William Henniker, did. Hearing the tirades screamed at the child through the bedroom wall, and seeing the poor, bedrag-

The Kidders lived in the old Cinque Port of Hythe, and this view features the town's attractive High Street. Marlinova Collection

gled child locked out in all weathers, he went to the police. Frances was hauled up in front of Hythe Magistrates, fined and ordered to send Louisa to live with a guardian.

Regrettably, some time later, Louisa was returned to her father because he was unable to keep up the payments to her guardian. The child's return to what had already become a strained household intensified Frances's hatred of her. The beatings recommenced almost immediately; however, this time William Kidder was not prepared to stand by and do nothing. After discovering his daughter had undergone a particularly savage beating from his wife, he threw Frances out of the house and would not let her in until the following morning.

In July 1867 Frances suffered a serious accident that was said to have aggravated her already cruel personality. While she was driving her husband's potato wagon the horse bolted, throwing her onto the ground. Her clothing became entangled in a wheel and she was dragged along for some distance causing injuries to her face, arm and leg. Some have used the accident as an excuse for Frances's later actions, saying it unbalanced her mind. However, as we have seen, she was already a pretty wretched creature even before the accident.

Family friend Mary Burwell nursed Frances back to health. Mary was to witness at first hand Mrs Kidder's frightening attitude towards Louisa, and was also caught in the middle of a violent argument between William and Frances during which Mrs Kidder threatened to kill both her husband and Louisa.

Therefore it is perhaps surprising that once she had recovered from her injuries in August 1867 Frances was allowed to take her own daughter, Emma, and Louisa to stay with her parents on Romney Marsh. They arrived on Saturday, 17 August, but Frances was in a bad mood all week. On the following Saturday she told a neighbour, Mrs Eliza Evans, that she hated her stepdaughter and would soon be rid of her.

The last day of the holiday, Sunday 25 August, saw Frances in a particularly sullen mood. She refused to eat anything and then declined to accompany her parents on their usual Sunday-evening walk. Frances was left to look after her younger sister Rhoda, brother Charley, Louisa, Emma and a baby girl.

New Romney was the birthplace of Frances Kidder, and she was to return to the area to brutally murder her stepdaughter. *Marlinova Collection*

With her husband due shortly to take her and the children back to Hythe, Frances decided it was now or never to carry out her promise to rid herself of her hated stepdaughter once and for all. Taking Louisa aside, she asked her if she would like to visit a fair in New Romney and suggested that they both change into old clothes so as not to get dirty. Leaving the younger children in the care of Rhoda, Frances took Louisa towards New Romney. However, they were never to reach the town, for as they approached Cobb's Bridge Frances carried out her plan and drowned Louisa in the ditch that ran under the bridge.

Back at the Turner house, Frances's parents had arrived home to find the children left alone. John Turner went out to look for his daughter and Louisa but was unable to find them. Upon returning to the house, he met William Kidder, who had arrived to take Frances and Louisa home. The two men decided on another search, although they went different ways in the hope of more success.

Finding nothing, William Kidder returned to the house. He was engaged in conversation with Mrs Turner when Frances came in, alone and very wet. She was immediately questioned as to the whereabouts of Louisa and after telling her husband, 'I don't want to see you' remained silent when asked if she had killed her. Upon being asked again Frances mumbled she had taken the child to meet her mother, before running upstairs.

When John Turner returned he went upstairs with William to question Frances about Louisa. By this time she had changed into dry clothes and was sitting on a box in her parents' bedroom. However, she refused to say anything at all regarding the evening's events. Feeling they had no other choice, the two men went to the police and returned with PC Aspinall. Frances repeated to him that she had not killed Louisa, but said the child had fallen into a ditch after being frightened by horses. She had attempted to rescue her and that's why she had come home all wet. She then told the police officer where the body could be found.

Aspinall then removed Frances to the police station on suspicion of murder and locked her in a cell. Taking Turner and Kidder with him, he then went to the *Ship* inn and gathered up volunteers to look for the missing girl. Her body was discovered around twenty minutes later lying in a foot of water by Cobb's Bridge, and was carried back to the inn.

The inquest on the death of Louisa Kidder Staples was held the next day at New Romney Town Hall before Mr W.D. Walker. William Kidder gave evidence and said his wife had been 'strange

Volunteers from the *Ship* inn in New Romney helped to look for the missing girl. Marlinova Collection

in the head' ever since the accident. John and Rhoda Turner and PC Aspinall were also called to testify. A surgeon named Wood confirmed that Louisa had died from drowning.

On the resumption of the inquest on the following Tuesday, a fifteen-year-old girl named Jane Smith revealed that Louisa had told her three days before her death that she knew that her step-mother was planning to kill her. She also told Miss Smith that Frances had tried to strangle her the previous evening and showed her some marks on her neck. The child was also threatened with being drowned in a ditch.

Mrs Evans then gave further evidence of Mrs Kidder's hatred towards her stepdaughter. She claimed Frances had told her, 'I mean to get rid of her before I get home; I hate the very sight of her,' and said William hated his daughter just as much as she did. She further added, 'I do not like other people's bastards.'

Corporal Isaac Sage, based at the School of Musketry in Hythe and a brother-in-law of Louisa's real mother, said he frequently saw the child with black eyes and bruises given to her by Frances Kidder.

Following just a quarter-of-an-hour of deliberation, the jury returned a verdict of wilful murder against the prisoner.

On Wednesday, 28 August 1867 Mrs Kidder appeared before

the magistrates' court, where she gave her version of Sunday's events:

I had no thoughts of doing such a thing as you say I have. I went halfway down to the seaside; I turned and came back again across the fields; I got as far as Mr Cobb's bridge and got halfway across it when two horses came up running as fast as they could. The child ran along the bank and then fell in. I heard her go in and I then jumped in to try and save her but she was farther along than where I went in. I screamed for help but no one came. I was some time before I got out and when I did get out I ran home as fast as I could and told my mother what had happened. While I was going home I did not see anyone. I had no thoughts of doing such a thing; I had been laid up and brought the child down for a change along with myself. We walked down from Hythe and it was dark nearly all the way down; it was nearly eleven o'clock before we got here. I should not have stayed so long at Romney but I expected my husband down. He knew where I was gone but he never liked me to come down here at all. I have always done my best for them all. He [William Kidder] *always said if he got half a chance he would serve me out and tell any lie against me. He once ill-used me very much and locked me out of doors. I had him up for it and he has been against me ever since. His child has been with me two years; I did my best for her in getting her clothes and keeping her clean and sending her to school. I could not do as I would have done because I had not the means; he would not let me have a farthing. The clothes I have I had before I had him. Gentlemen I call it heart-breaking to anyone to come up and tell the same as that girl* [Jane Smith] *did; for I never knew her and never spoke to her. Also, that soldier* [Corporal Sage] *saying he came to my house to tea, which I never saw him before. I have always kept myself respectable before I was married and I have more so since, for my living. I never did any one any harm nor wished them any. I have endeavoured to do my best by everyone and if I could help my friends I have always done so. I have only been out two nights since I have been here and then I was out with my father and mother. I have not been out since till Sunday night last when I went out to meet them. I never cared to go out here, I wanted to get home again and I was expecting my husband down; that is why I stayed so long before I went out that evening. I have nothing more to say.*

The prisoner was committed for trial at Maidstone Assizes and was transported to the County Town the next day, although the journey was delayed when Frances suffered a fit at Ashford police station. However, as there was no Kent Winter Assizes, Frances spent the next six months in Maidstone Gaol awaiting her trial. William declined to visit her and began an affair with his wife's younger sister, who was staying with him on the pretext of looking after baby Emma.

The trial finally began at Maidstone Crown Court on Thursday, 12 March 1868 before Mr Justice Byles. Mr Biron and Mr Dering represented the prosecution and Mr Channell defended the prisoner. Mary Burwell was amongst those who gave evidence and related how she saw the prisoner throw Louisa against a wall, causing a lump on her head almost the size of an egg. On another occasion she saw Frances beat the girl and emerge with her pinafore covered in blood.

William Henniker told the court he often took the child in when she was locked out and looked after her until William Kidder returned to the house. Frances's sister Mary related that her sister told her Louisa would not be returning to Hythe from New Romney as she 'meant to take it out in the fields and drown it in front of the house'. Caroline Page and Edmund Walters both gave evidence that they had seen Frances with Louisa that Sunday evening, while Mary Fagg claimed to have heard a muffled cry from near Cobb's Bridge.

Frances herself stuck by her story of Louisa drowning after the horses had caused her to fall into the ditch. Her defence counsel tried to secure sympathy from the jury by making play of her husband's abandonment of the prisoner since she was sent for trial. He also alleged that many of the prosecution witnesses' statements were exaggerated and there was no definite case of murder to answer; the accident could not be disproved.

Following the judge's summing up, the jury took only twelve minutes to reach its verdict – Guilty. A plea to the Home Secretary to commute the sentence to imprisonment failed and the date of the execution was set for 2 April 1868.

During the three weeks leading up to her execution, Frances finally felt at some kind of peace with herself. This was largely due to the kindness shown her by the prison chaplain, the Reverend Sugden Frazer. As Frances was unable to write, he also wrote several letters for her to her husband. William, who had not seen his wife since her arrest, came to visit her, but as usual they had a falling out, this time over his relationship with her sister. On a second visit he confessed to the affair, which resulted in Frances violently shouting and shrieking and William fleeing the prison.

Later that same day, Frances heard the gallows for her execution being erected and calmed down as she realised that the end was near. William Calcraft, the official hangman, was to carry out the execution. His short drop method of hanging, using only two to three feet of rope so causing his charge to slowly strangle, was much criticised, as was his drinking. Charles Dickens, who saw him at work, was one such critic. Thomas Hardy was another and was so greatly affected by seeing a woman hanged by Calcraft when he was sixteen he is thought to have based his book *Tess of the d'Urbervilles* on it. Nevertheless, William Calcraft was to serve as executioner for forty-five years until he was forced to retire in 1874.

On the morning of her execution, Frances was visited by Reverend Sugden Frazer and after taking breakfast accompanied him to the prison chapel. However, when Frazer left her she began screaming and could not be quietened until he returned. He wrote two final letters for her; one to her parents asking for forgiveness for her crime, and the other to her husband, which was hand-delivered. Kidder returned his reply personally and then joined the crowd of around 2,000 that had gathered around the gallows outside the main gate of the gaol.

As twelve o'clock approached, Calcraft, along with the prison governor, Major Bannister, and Mr Furley, the under-sheriff, made their way to the condemned cell. Frances was asked to stand and she was pinioned by having her hands tied together and her arms strapped to her side. A prayer was said with Frazer and she leaned on his arm as they walked to the scaffold. The chaplain led the way up the steps, but Frances became hysterical and needed to be supported to the drop by two prison warders. As she muttered her last prayer she was heard to say, 'Lord Jesus forgive me'. The hood was then placed over her head and as the bolt to the trap door was drawn she cried, 'Jesus!' The body plunged three feet and could be seen moving violently above the black cloth that surrounded the gallows. Screams were heard amongst the crowd and some were said to have fainted. Only after several minutes had elapsed did the body become still. The corpse was left to hang for one hour before being taken down. Later that day it was laid to rest within the prison walls.

The troubled soul of Frances Kidder was finally at peace, although for her husband she had one last sting in the tail. The hanging had obviously elicited some sympathy for the poor woman amongst the crowd and following the proceedings a mob of around 300 people followed William Kidder home. An effigy of him was burned in the street and windows were broken, leading to a large police presence to prevent further disturbances.

CHAPTER 8

A Moment of Madness

Dover, 1868

The county of Kent holds not only the dubious distinction of having the last woman to be publicly hanged, but also that of having the first person to be privately executed after the passing of the Capital Punishment Within Prisons Bill. Some four months after Frances Kidder's very public hanging, young Thomas Wells was to have a much more private affair.

Thomas Wells was a dreamy nineteen-year-old who was rather immature and childish for his age. He liked nothing better than to play tricks on his family at their home in Round Tower Street, Dover and then blame them on his younger brother. His fishmonger father later claimed he was often 'given way to gusts of passion'. One particular passion for Wells was his girlfriend, to whom he was devoted. They were engaged to be married, despite her misgivings over Wells's mood swings, which were quite pronounced. One minute he could be sweet and gentle, the next moody and argumentative. The 'gusts of passion' could often be interpreted as fits of temper. Perhaps Wells was influenced by the illustrated police sheet newspapers that he relished, with their details of shocking crimes and court reports. He had fantasies of being a criminal himself and was known to have acquired his own gun, which was his pride and joy.

However, back in the real world, Wells was employed as a carriage cleaner by the London, Chatham and Dover Railway and was based at Dover Priory station. He had been taken on about eighteen months previously and initially showed himself to be a helpful and willing worker. The superintendent of the station, Edward Adolphus Walshe, had taken the young man under his wing and was quite fond of him. Although a strict disciplinarian, Walshe was essentially a kindly man and was well respected by both railway staff and townsfolk alike.

Unfortunately, in the summer of 1867, Wells suffered an accident, which seemed to affect his personality. As he was passing between a carriage and an engine he became trapped between the buffers. He was found in a semi-conscious state and was taken home, where he was treated for head and neck injuries.

Within a few days, however, Wells was back at work, although he appeared to have acquired a far more sullen personality. He also became lazy and unreliable and was constantly warned by Walshe over his conduct. In April 1868 the two men had a falling out when Walshe asked Wells to collect a cartful of manure and take it to the station house for use on his garden. Wells (perhaps rightly) initially refused to do it because it was not part of his job, but upon being threatened with dismissal he reluctantly carried out the task.

A few days later, on 30 April, Wells decided to take his gun, an old-fashioned type using gunpowder and percussion caps, to work. He spent his rest period firing at targets within the station yard, but the great noise produced by the gun boomed around the neighbourhood. Walshe went to confront Wells and found him in the porters' room. Blazing with anger, he told Wells not to bring the gun to work and then stormed angrily out of the room.

In front of the others in the room, Wells countered, 'I will let the old bugger have the contents of this'. Engine driver John Prescott told him not to be such a fool, whereupon Wells replied, 'I will let the old bugger have it'.

Within a short time Walshe returned to the room and asked Wells what he had done with the gun. Lying through his teeth, Wells told him he had thrown it away, but the still-agitated Walshe insisted he would have to report the matter to Henry Cox, the Senior Superintendent for the Dover area.

At this moment, the evening express from London pulled into the station. Both Wells and Walshe left the room and Wells climbed into the brake van, as it was his job to travel down with the train to the Harbour station and clean the carriages before the return trip to London.

Walshe remained on the platform to see the train off, but as it began to enter the tunnel at the end of the station, Wells jumped from the brake van and walked over to him. When Walshe asked him why he had done this Wells remarked he did not like to be made a fool of. By now thoroughly exasperated, Walshe retorted that he had no alternative but to report the matter to his superior.

On the following day (1 May), Wells began his shift at 6.30 a.m. working in the carriage shed. He was still brooding over the events of the previous day, as he told twelve-year-old Charles Sinclair of the loco department, 'If that old bugger says much more to me today I'll shoot him'.

Sinclair later said he did not take the threat seriously as he presumed it was just bravado. However, during the morning, Wells skipped off work for ten minutes so he could purchase 4d worth of gunpowder from Messrs Smythe & Co.'s ironmongers in Snargate Street.

Later that morning, Wells was summoned to the station office to face Henry Cox and Edward Walshe. He was presented with an ultimatum: if he showed contrition the matter would be forgotten, but if he refused to apologise he would face a fine or dismissal. He was given ten minutes to think it over.

Wells left the office and went outside, where he met John Golder, a station porter. He told him that if he was going to be dismissed 'Walshe would know about it'.

When the ten minutes was up Wells returned to the station office, but had no intention of grasping the olive branch offered to him. He remained surly and aggressive and offered no apologies for his actions. Wells was then asked to leave the office once more while Cox and Walshe decided what punishment should be handed out to him.

As the two men started to discuss what to do, Wells barged

A Victorian view of Snargate Street, Dover, where Thomas Wells purchased the gunpowder to carry out his deadly deed. Bob Hollingsbee

Dover Priory station in the 1860s, where Thomas Wells shot stationmaster Edward Walshe in cold blood. Bob Hollingsbee

back into the room, this time holding the gun. He walked over to Walshe, pointed the gun at his head and from point-blank range fired it. The ball entered the front of Walshe's head and passed out through the back, completely shattering the skull and killing him straight away.

Wells calmly turned around and walked out of the room. He was seen by John Golder leaving the office and running towards the carriage sheds.

The startled and dumbstruck Cox ran outside and called out to a gang of platelayers for assistance. He instructed one of them to fetch the police, another to find a surgeon and the rest to look for Wells. Upon the arrival of Superintendent John Coram and Sergeant George Stevens of Dover Police they were taken to the carriage sheds, where they found Wells sitting in a second-class carriage. He offered no resistance and calmly allowed himself to be handcuffed before he was taken off to the police station, where he was charged with the murder of Edward Walshe.

The unfortunate Walshe was laid to rest in Brompton Cemetery, London on 7 May 1868. A subscription was set up for his widow, but her application to the cash-strapped LCDR for a pension was refused.

Wells's trial before Justice Willis at Maidstone Assizes was a
foregone conclusion, and the jury took only five minutes to find
him guilty. The only defence offered was that Wells was
temporarily insane owing to the accident that had happened
nearly a year before. Wells was sentenced to hang and taken to the
condemned cell at Maidstone Gaol.

The execution of Wells was to be the first in Britain to take
place within prison walls following the passing of the *Capital
Punishments Act* in May, which had abolished public executions.
The date set for the hanging was Thursday, 13 August 1868 and
in the meantime a permanent set of gallows was erected in the
former exercise yard. This was hidden from public view by high
walls, and for additional security an iron roof was built over the
scaffold, which was hidden from the prying eyes of the inmates by
movable shutters.

Wells passed the time by writing over a hundred letters. Pleas
for forgiveness were sent to Henry Cox and Mrs Walshe and
gushing love letters flowed to his 'intended' expressing sorrow for
his actions and hoping that one day they would marry in heaven.
The young lady came to see him in gaol, as did his father, two
sisters and two aunts from his close-knit family. The prison chaplain, the Reverend Sugden Frazer (who had comforted Frances
Kidder just a few months previously) was on hand to offer
support to the heartbroken relatives. However, during his last visit
on the afternoon before the execution, Wells's father broke down
completely and had to be carried away in a fit. On seeing this,
Wells himself became hysterical, but he later calmed down and
had a restful night.

The prisoner arose early on the morning of his execution, and
after a light breakfast partook of Holy Communion. He remained
dressed in the same LCDR porters' uniform he had worn since his
arrest. As the 10.30 time for his execution approached he became
hysterical once more. However, he composed himself in time for
the arrival of the executioner, William Calcraft, and his assistant
George Smith, a cattle dealer and hangman for the Midland
counties. They pinioned the prisoner by tying his arms and hands
together and Chaplain Frazer and prison officials escorted him to
the scaffold. The *Dover Chronicle* vividly described Wells's final
moments:

> *Now, as he stood there, helpless in the hands of his executioners, one
> could not help pitying him. He appeared to be almost unconscious,
> and before he left his cell, brandy and sal volatile had to be
> administered to him. His elbows were strapped close to his sides, and*

The front cover of the *Illustrated Police News* recording the execution of Thomas Wells. Marlinova Collection

his wrists were also bound up in strong leather thongs. His shoulders, either from the strapping, or else from the fright of the victim, were elevated to his ears, and his face, which on the day of the trial was so composed, was now distorted by fear; his lips were parched, and terribly swollen, his eyes were fixed upon vacancy, and over his countenance was suffused a most ghastly vivid colour. The chaplain stood in front of him, grasping the lad's clasped hands, and praying with a fervency that affected all present.

Wells seemed to hear the prayers, for his lips every now and then moved, and a low mumbling sound was heard. While all this was

William Calcraft, the executioner of both Frances Kidder and Thomas Wells.
Marlinova Collection

going on, the two hangmen were silently making every arrangement. Calcraft, so soon as Wells, supported on either side by a warder, was in the centre of the drop, fixed the noose around his neck, quickly, but taking care that the knot should press under the ear; and Smith, kneeling down, passed a strap round the legs of the condemned man, and tightly buckled them together. Directly Wells felt the rope around his neck, he moistened his lips, and with difficulty commenced singing. The chaplain stopped praying, and, amid a silence broken only by the shuffling of the hangmen, Wells sang:

> *Happy soul, thy days are ended,*
> *All thy mourning days below,*
> *Go, by angel friends attended,*
> *To the throne of Jesus go.*

The hymn was one he came across in one of the prison books, and he sang it several times during the two or three days that immediately preceded the execution. The words of the first two lines were distinctly heard by the group of spectators, but when he had got so far the white cap was drawn over the quivering face, and the voice was so muffled that the remaining words were inaudible. But the verse was finished. The lips could be seen moving under the cap, and a low sound reached the bystanders. Then someone made a sign to Calcraft, who pressed Wells's clasped hands in his own, stepped to the back of the drop, and motioned to Smith, who stood on the steps leading underneath, his right hand grasping a lever. What followed is soon told. There was a rusty grating noise, that jarred terribly on the ears of those present, a dull thud from the heavy trap door falling against the sack of straw that had been placed there to prevent its rebounding, and the soul of Thomas Wells was swung into Eternity.

CHAPTER 9

Cut-throat at the Camp

Shorncliffe Camp, 1875

The ever-present threat of tough discipline and rampant bullying at the large Shorncliffe army camp (situated just outside Folkestone) in Victorian times inevitably led to the minds of many soldiers tipping over the edge. Suicides were rife and fights an everyday occurrence, but the murder of Joe Foulston by his friend John Morgan was certainly not expected. These two men had served together in the army for a number of years and were great pals, and seemingly on good terms just minutes before the murder occurred, so what made John Morgan do it?

Both Joe Foulston and John Morgan were bandsmen in the 82nd (Prince of Wales's Volunteers) Regiment of Foot stationed at Shorncliffe Camp. They were among the thirty-two men stationed in an overcrowded and unsanitary single hut in 'A' line, one of 192 wooden huts that had been hastily erected during the Crimean War for the British German Legion.

During the evening of Saturday, 6 March 1875, all but three of the bandsmen in the hut were out enjoying the hostelries in Folkestone, Cheriton and Sandgate. Left in the hut were both Joe Foulston and John Morgan, along with John Reader, and two young brothers named Henry and Alfred Simpson, who were bandsboys. All appeared calm in the hut with Reader flat out on his bed in an intoxicated state, Foulston reading a book and Morgan assisting the brothers in preparing supper. Foulston and Morgan frequently spoke to each other and appeared to be on good terms, which made what happened next all the more baffling.

With supper almost ready, Morgan asked one of the brothers to go and fetch him some sweets, and then just a minute later asked the other one to run after his brother to ask him to buy some sauce to make the supper taste better. The second brother was most reluctant to leave the hut, but upon seeing the menace on Morgan's face thought the better of it and went on his way. As he walked away from the hut, he turned around and noticed Morgan standing on a bedstead looking at him through the top window.

In the next hut along the line, the atmosphere was of a far more boisterous nature as a number of the men were noisily enjoying a game of cards. However, all of their cheerful jollity was suddenly cut short when they saw the horrifying sight of Joe Foulston staggering through the door covered in blood. A closer inspection of the poor man revealed that he had suffered a number of deep gashes to the throat, exposing the backbone, and severe cuts to his hands and face. Almost immediately, a wet towel was bound tightly around his throat in an effort to stem the heavy flow of blood.

Yet amazingly, in spite of his horrific injuries, Foulston tried to communicate with the men, who initially suspected he had attempted to commit suicide. He pointed to a piece of paper and a pen, and while being held up by two of the men shakily managed to write 'John Morgan done this, just now'. Some of the men went next-door to fetch Morgan, who was seen stooping over a pail of water washing his face and hands. However, he steadfastly refused to leave the hut until a sergeant ordered him to, and then was marched into the adjoining hut. There, the clearly dying Foulston managed to point at Morgan before lapsing into unconsciousness. Within a few minutes he perished from a heavy loss of blood.

Morgan was taken to the guardroom, where it was noticed that his clothes were covered with blood. After being cautioned, he was ordered to change before being handed over to the police.

A search of the hut where the alleged horrible deed took place revealed a very gory sight. While Reader still amazingly slept on, pools of blood could be seen either side of an overturned table, and a line of blood and body tissue traced every step taken by the unfortunate Foulston into the adjoining hut. A bloodstained razor lying on the floor was assumed, in all probability, to have been used to inflict the terrible injuries.

The deceased man was thirty-three years of age at the time of his death, having served twenty years in the army, mainly in India. He was a member of the East India Company before serving in the 105th and 7th Foot regiments. In 1868 he joined the 82nd, and in July 1874 the regiment was relocated to Shorncliffe upon their return from India. He was known as a gentle man who was very popular amongst his comrades. His piccolo-playing was also said to be first-rate.

Morgan, on the other hand, was a rather sallow young man of nineteen who had followed his father into the same regiment as a very young bandsboy. He had served with Joe Foulston in India and had apparently got on very well with him.

The preliminary hearing of the murder charge against Morgan took place in Hythe just two days after the killing; although there was a one-and-a-half-hour delay in starting the proceedings while a medical witness was despatched from Shorncliffe. At the hearing, the prisoner displayed a remarkable composure that seemed to either indicate a consciousness of his innocence or a failure to comprehend the dreadful penalty that hung over him. He cross-examined some of the witnesses himself, but seemed unwilling to press for answers that may have been favourable to his defence.

During his evidence, army surgeon Dr Alexander Turner gave a chilling account of the serious nature of the neck wounds and ruled out that the deceased could have inflicted them himself, thereby dispelling the opinion held by many that Foulston had committed suicide. Dr Turner also confirmed that the razor was

The accommodation huts at Shorncliffe Camp. It was in one such hut that John Morgan cut the throat of Joe Foulston. Marlinova Collection

The tented accommodation on St Martins Plain, Shorncliffe Camp, with an inspection taking place. Marlinova Collection

indeed the most likely murder weapon. The proceedings were concluded after the prisoner was committed for trial at Maidstone Assizes later that week.

The unfortunate Joe Foulston was buried at Wednesday, 10 March with full military honours. On the next day the jury at Maidstone was out for only half an hour before finding John Morgan guilty of the murder of Joe Foulston, and the judge duly passed the sentence of death on the prisoner. However, the very speed of the events that led to the sentence of death being passed only five days after the murder was committed meant that Morgan had been sentenced to death before the inquiry into the death of Joe Foulston had been concluded!

Nevertheless, the jury at the inquiry reached the same verdict as their counterparts in Maidstone: that John Morgan had murdered Joe Foulston, and added they thought the whole inquest had been a farce!

Following his conviction, Morgan confessed his guilt to the chaplain at Maidstone Gaol, but still refused to give a reason why he had perpetrated such a dreadful deed on an old friend.

Shorncliffe Military Cemetery, a peaceful haven of serenity for those victims of violence at Shorncliffe Camp. Marlinova Collection

Nevertheless, as the date of his execution approached, he began to express deep remorse at what he had done. Two days before he was due to die, he had a last tearful meeting with his old soldier father and asked him to give some photographs of himself taken at the gaol to his comrades at the camp.

Morgan was said to have met his end bravely when hanged on the morning of Tuesday, 23 March 1875.

CHAPTER 10

Under the Influence

Hythe, 1875

Those unfortunate enough to reside in the rundown Rose & Crown Cottages off the High Street in Hythe were not the only ones to be habitually 'under the influence'. The town's tiny police force had a reputation for drunkenness and incompetence that was second to none; with the Superintendent being the worst culprit of all! Matters were brought to a head in 1875, following the death of a hawker in the cottages.

The four *Rose & Crown* cottages were a nasty stain on the respectability of Hythe. Situated between the High Street and Chapel Street, they were let by the landlord of the *Rose & Crown* and were described as being in a 'dingy and dilapidated condition and a disgrace to the borough to whose principal street they are in such close proximity'. Consequently, the only takers for the cottages were usually life's unfortunates such as travelling hawkers and tramps, who were prepared to put up with the adjoining slaughterhouse, pig sties and open privy, whose drains ran in front of the cottages.

However 58-year-old travelling hawker Charles Rendle wasn't fussy and in the late autumn of 1874 moved into one of the cottages with Ann Ponten, a year his senior. Although not married, they had lived together as 'man and wife' for around thirty years. Most of the couple's time appeared to be spent in the adjoining pub spending what little they earned on getting drunk.

On many of their drinking forays Rendle and Ponten were accompanied by an equally downtrodden couple named Parlett, who lived next-door. However, when the couples were not drinking together they were usually fighting. Rendle sported scratches on his face caused during an argument with the Parletts after he had accused them of stealing money from him. Nevertheless, this appeared to be forgotten as the four of them tumbled into the *Rose & Crown* during the morning of Wednesday, 10 March 1875 and proceeded to spend the rest of the day there. The marathon drinking session continued into

Thursday, but by early evening, with all four of them hopelessly drunk, Mrs Bailey, the landlady, decided they should leave. Rendle, in particular, objected to this and made his feelings clear, whereupon Mrs Bailey proceeded to floor him, twice! He was then bundled out of the pub along with the others, although Ann Ponten also made her feelings known and put up some resistance.

In fact, Ann Ponten was determined not to take the scuffle lying down and went to the police station to complain that Mrs Bailey had assaulted her 'husband'. Police Superintendent George Raymond sent PC James Harman round to the *Rose & Crown* at 7 p.m. to investigate the disturbance. When he visited Ann Ponten at her cottage to hear her side of the story he found her fast asleep on her bed.

A blacksmith named Edward Watches, who lived next-door but one to Rendle and Ponten, later claimed he had been awoken by the couple arguing later that evening, at around 11 p.m. Furthermore, he had heard the sound of a fall, although the Parletts (who lived closer) said they heard nothing.

The *Rose & Crown Inn* in Hythe High Street. The body of Ann Ponten was found in the cottages that stood behind the inn. Marlinova Collection

On the following morning, at 5 a.m., Watches heard more arguing and, upon returning from his breakfast, saw Rendle in the tap room of the *Rose & Crown*. The hawker proceeded to spend most of the day in the pub, but there was no sign of Ann Ponten. Rendle later left the pub for a time to go to his cottage; however, he later returned to tell the landlord that his 'wife' was dead.

The police were called for and Raymond and Harman arrived at Rendle's cottage at 11 p.m. They found it in pitch darkness, yet through the gloom they saw Rendle sitting quietly and a woman lying dead on the bed; her clothes had obviously been rearranged.

Hythe surgeon John Hackney was sent for and he found a bruise the size of a sixpence on the forehead of the deceased and foaming at the mouth and nose. The bruise appeared to be the cause of the death. Rendle claimed he knew nothing of her death until he woke up and found her dead. He said the bruise had occurred after Ann Ponten had fallen over during a drunken stupor.

Nevertheless, Raymond arrested him on the charge that he had assaulted and killed Ann Ponten. On the following day Rendle appeared before the Borough Police Court, where John Hackney confirmed that Ann Ponten's death could have been caused by either a blow to the head or a fall. Mary Parlett revealed that she had seen the bruise on Ponten when she met her on the Friday morning, although she thought it was smaller in size then. This evidence, coupled with Edward Watches's statement that he had heard an argument and the sound of a fall coming from Rendle's cottage, appeared to prove that Rendle had assaulted and killed Ann Ponten.

However, it was not that clear cut, for another possible cause of death was revealed during the inquest at Hythe Town Hall. Ann Hobbs, a servant in the employ of Mrs Bailey, revealed that when her employer threw the drunken foursome out of the pub, she pushed Ann Ponten down on to the brick road, where she could have hit her head. Mary Parlett was on hand to give evidence once again, but had been so drunk she claimed she couldn't remember a thing.

The evidence as to the cause of death of Ann Ponten was clearly inconclusive and the jury ruled that she had died from extravasation of blood on the brain caused by a blow or fall. Rendle was set free, although he was warned that he would be rearrested if further evidence came to light.

Whether Charles Rendle (directly) or Mrs Bailey (indirectly) was the cause of Ann Ponten's death will never be known; and Hythe Police appeared uninterested to find out more. The force's attitude was typical of the way it was being led at the time by the corrupt and unpopular George Raymond, who was himself often drunk, and bullied his subordinates. At the time of the Ponten case in March 1875 he was in charge of three full-time constables (James Harman and PCs Aedy and Gauntlett) plus three part-time constables. Raymond was responsible to a Watch Committee, which consisted of the mayor, Alderman Taylor, plus councillors Cobay, Cobb, Court, Halke, Horton and Wood.

PC James Harman, who had investigated the Ponten death with Raymond, was often on the receiving end of his bullying and drunken behaviour. He had joined the Hythe force in October 1874 but by June 1875, three months after the fracas at the *Rose & Crown*, he had had enough. He lodged an official complaint with the Watch Committee on account of Raymond's drunkenness on duty and tyrannical behaviour. Aedy and Gauntlett supported him in his allegations. In return Raymond reported the three constables for neglect of duty.

An inquiry was held by the Watch Committee, which found:

a state of mismanagement and insubordination in the police force utterly incompatible with the proper discharge of their duties and, without dwelling upon the strongly conflicting evidence...they have determined to make an entire change and thereby call upon the whole force to resign.

So the whole force, including Raymond, was sacked. His fate had been effectively sealed when old Harry Wear, the town's lamplighter, was called upon and he related, 'I have seen Raymond lots of times drunk – sozzled as that fiddler's bitch. Sir, he was; every time I saw him he stank of beer.'

For the next three months, it appears Hythe was without a police force of any kind, but in August Raymond was inexplicably reappointed and so was Aedy (presumably the two of them had made up). Gauntlett was also reinstated following a petition signed by the town's ratepayers, although he was soon discharged on 14 August suffering from nervous debility. Harman was, unsurprisingly, not reinstated, and Thomas Thompson took his position.

However, Raymond's reinstatement failed to alter his ways: if anything his egotistical feeling that he was indispensable made him far worse. Thompson soon resigned in 1876 due to Raymond's drunken behaviour, and brought to the Watch Committee's attention their superintendent's habit of visiting public houses and obtaining free drinks. Nothing was done, however. Yet if Raymond discovered that one of his constables had had a drink on duty he had them hauled up before the Watch Committee, where they were fined or dismissed – a classic case of double standards!

An example of Raymond's treachery occurred during the summer of 1877. He had spent the day with PC Bates visiting pubs in the High Street before they slept off their intoxicated state by the bank of the Royal Military Canal. Raymond awoke first, and thirty minutes later returned with another officer to arrest Bates! The unfortunate constable (along with PC Laker) was hauled before the Watch Committee and sacked.

When Raymond was reported again in February 1878 for being drunk on duty, the Watch Committee was now led by Mr Mackeson, owner of the brewery in the town, who was prepared to take a much tougher line on discipline. In addition, he was not in a good mood the day Raymond appeared before the committee; having been slashed earlier in the day with a horsewhip wielded by a gypsy named William Daisy. George Raymond, the police

The Royal Military Canal in Hythe, where the town's policemen in the 1870s liked to sleep off their alcoholic excesses. *Marlinova Collection*

officer who thought he was above the law, was finally dismissed for good and replaced by Aedy. From that day the Hythe Police Force finally gained some respectability, and in 1889 it was absorbed into the Kent County Force.

The *Rose & Crown* cottages were later demolished as slums, and the truth of what really happened to Ann Ponten was lost with them.

CHAPTER 11

The Unpopular Hero

Dover, 1876

There's no denying that Charles Wooden was a brave soldier: amongst his many battle honours was the award of no less than a Victoria Cross. Unfortunately, his rather cold and aloof manner meant that he never gained the popularity and respect amongst his peers that his valour deserved. Even his VC was issued only grudgingly and after protest. Shunned and unloved, the troubled lancer was to meet a suitably bizarre end.

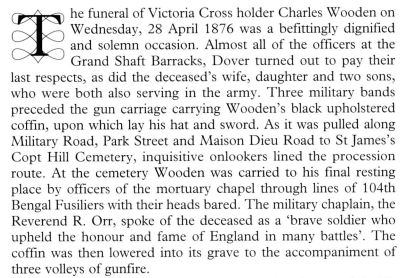he funeral of Victoria Cross holder Charles Wooden on Wednesday, 28 April 1876 was a befittingly dignified and solemn occasion. Almost all of the officers at the Grand Shaft Barracks, Dover turned out to pay their last respects, as did the deceased's wife, daughter and two sons, who were both also serving in the army. Three military bands preceded the gun carriage carrying Wooden's black upholstered coffin, upon which lay his hat and sword. As it was pulled along Military Road, Park Street and Maison Dieu Road to St James's Copt Hill Cemetery, inquisitive onlookers lined the procession route. At the cemetery Wooden was carried to his final resting place by officers of the mortuary chapel through lines of 104th Bengal Fusiliers with their heads bared. The military chaplain, the Reverend R. Orr, spoke of the deceased as a 'brave soldier who upheld the honour and fame of England in many battles'. The coffin was then lowered into its grave to the accompaniment of three volleys of gunfire.

If only Charles Wooden had been appreciated as much in life as in death it could all have ended so differently. Born in 1826 and of German descent, Wooden enrolled in the 17th Lancers (Duke of Cambridge's Own) in 1845. He proved himself to be a good soldier and in 1854 was promoted to sergeant major. However, as a handler of men, Wooden proved to be less capable. His strong German accent made communication difficult and led his colleagues to regard him as aloof. Others thought him plain 'queer' and put it down to his constant exposure to the sun when

Charles Wooden VC, a most unpopular hero who was to meet a tragic end.
Marlinova Collection

he served in India. They mockingly nicknamed him 'Tish me, the Devil' because he had said this to the sentry on duty one night when in a drunken state.

On the outbreak of the Crimean War in 1854, Wooden was sent to Russia as part of the ill-fated Light Brigade of Calvary and became involved in the infamous charge at Balaclava on 25 October 1854. Of the 145 men of the 17th Lancers who took part in the battle only two officers and thirty-seven men survived. Wooden was one of those fortunate few, although he had had a close shave when his horse was shot out from under him.

The Commanding Officer of the 17th Lancers, Captain William Morris, had been left badly wounded on the battlefield following a most extraordinary sequence of events. During the charge on the Russian Hussars, Morris went for their leader and ran him through with his sword with such force he was unable to pull it out. During the effort to free his sword, he fell off his horse and was surrounded by the enemy, who attacked with sabres before taking him prisoner. However, during the confusion of the battle, Morris was able to escape and, pursued by the Russians, rode off on a horse. The severity of his wounds caused him to fall off, and although he managed to grab another horse this one was shot out from under him. The fallen animal landed on his leg and Morris lapsed into unconsciousness. When he came to, he managed to free the leg and, despite having a broken right arm, broken ribs and deep cuts to the head, made his way towards the British lines. On the way, Morris came across the body of Captain Nolan, who had led the charge as misdirected by Lord Lucan. Morris and Nolan had been close friends and had exchanged letters before the battle. Upon seeing his dead friend Morris lapsed back into unconsciousness and lay on the field of battle throughout the night. In the morning he was spotted, but an attempt by Turkish troops to recover the two bodies foundered when they fled the field during sustained Russian gunfire.

The few surviving members of the cavalry were then asked to attempt a rescue and Wooden volunteered his services along with James Mouat, a surgeon in the 6th Dragoons. Under heavy fire, they made their way out to where Morris lay, and after dressing his wounds brought him back to the British lines. Thanks to the bravery of the two men, Morris was able to make a full recovery. He continued to serve in the army, but died four years later in India.

Mouat was honoured for his heroism in February 1857 when he was one of the original eighty-five men awarded the Victoria Cross. He later rose up through the ranks to become Surgeon General Sir James Mouat KBC VC. Wooden's bravery was ignored, however, possibly because of his German origins. In recompense he was made Regimental Sergeant Major of the 17th Lancers, but the non-award of the VC greatly played on his mind and aggravated his prickly personality. Over and over in his mind he questioned why only Mouat had been honoured for a deed they had both performed. He decided to broach the matter with the army and wrote to Mouat asking for his support, which he promised to give. The army initially replied that they were 'very unwilling to bring any further claim for the Victoria Cross for an act performed at so distant a period.' Undeterred, Wooden continued to press his claim, and on 26 October 1858 the army reluctantly relented and awarded him his VC. His VC citation reads:

For having, after the retreat of the Light Cavalry, at the Battle of Balaclava, been instrumental, together with Dr James Mouat CB, in saving the life of Lieutenant Colonel Morris CB, of the 17th Lancers, by proceeding under heavy fire to his assistance, when he was lying very dangerously wounded in an exposed situation.

Any pleasure Wooden may have gained from the VC award was soon tempered by the attitude of his colleagues, who felt his persistence in asking for a VC went against the etiquette of the army. He became even less popular than before and in October 1860 was transferred as a commissioned quartermaster lieutenant to the 6th (Inniskilling) Dragoons. Wooden's offhand manner soon alienated his new his new comrades as well. To make matters worse, his new regiment was hit by a number of scandals during its spell in India under commanding officer Thomas Crawley. Wooden was forced to act as a witness in a number of courts martial and scandals, which led to him becoming even more out of favour.

Sick of the regiment's troubles, Wooden was transferred in

Dover's Grand Shaft Barracks, where VC hero Charles Wooden was found shot in the face. The photograph was taken in 1964, shortly before the buildings were demolished. Bob Hollingsbee

St James's Cemetery, Dover: the last resting place of Charles Wooden.
Marlinova Collection

1865 to the 5th Lancers, and then on to the 4th Bengal Fusiliers in 1871. They came to be billeted at the Grand Shaft Barracks in Dover, where Wooden lived with his wife and children. Unfortunately, Wooden found life in Dover utterly miserable. By now, the lack of respect from his colleagues, which had led to fifteen years without any kind of promotion, had turned him into a manic-depressive. He drank heavily and suffered from a number of medical problems, including severe headaches, the effects of sunstroke, neuralgia and, latterly, raging toothache. His problems only heightened his unpopularity with his men, several of whom had threatened to 'get him'.

Wooden finally lost his increasingly fragile hold on reality in mysterious circumstances on Monday, 26 April 1876. He was found slumped across his bed in a pool of blood and, still conscious, pointed to his mouth and said he wanted a tooth pulled out. When Dr Hooper examined the mouth he found that the whole of its roof was smashed. Wooden was taken to hospital, but died twelve hours later.

A coroner's inquest was held the following day in the barrack court-martial room. Dr Hooper expressed the opinion that Wooden had shot at his tooth in a bid to ease the pain. He had fired two shots: although the first had missed the mouth, the second bullet had gone through the top of the mouth and lodged itself in the brain, causing death. Wooden was known to have purchased a small breach-loading pocket pistol a few days previously and Mrs Wooden found it on the floor. When examined, the gun was found to contain an empty cartridge, and a box of the same cartridges was later found in his room.

Wooden's unpopularity was highlighted by the fact that only his batman, Private Richard Kirby, and two officers provided statements as to his character at the inquest. Not surprisingly, the jury returned the verdict that Wooden had shot himself 'while in a state of temporary insanity'. Others, however, disagreed, including Kirby, who did his best to defend his officer's honour. Although admitting Wooden was in pain with his toothache, he claimed his manner was normal on the day of the shooting and thought it most unlikely that such a brave soldier would have shot himself. Perhaps one of Wooden's many enemies carried out the deed, but the manner of the shooting makes this most unlikely. Thirty years of rejection had finally proved to be too much for the unpopular hero.

Postscript: In addition to the Victoria Cross, Charles Wooden also held a Crimea Medal (with bars Alma, Balaclava, Inkerman and Sebastopol), Turkish Medal, French War Medal and Indian Mutiny Medal. After his death, they passed to his son, who sold them along with his own medals in 1910. They returned to the family in 1926 when purchased by Wooden's grandson Sidney Herbert Wooden. They were sold again in 1972, and subsequently since; although the Victoria Cross was lost in the family and a replacement had to be obtained.

CHAPTER 12

The Mysterious Disappearance of Elizabeth Hearnden

Folkestone, 1884

Annie Johnson knew where ten-year-old Elizabeth Hearnden was, but she wasn't telling. Thirty-seven-year-old Miss Johnson ran a lodging house in Bouverie Road, Folkestone close to the Bouverie Hotel, yet it appears she was also engaged in a more serious pastime; that of acquiring young girls from poor families for use as house-maids and then selling them on to whoever was prepared to pay the going price.

iss Johnson had acquired Elizabeth Hearnden through her friend Sarah Marsh, who supplied her with logs from her home in Swingfield Minnis. Johnson, who was in the habit of taking in young girls to help around the house, had asked her friend if she knew anyone suitable and the young daughter of her friend Caroline Hearnden sprang to Mrs Marsh's mind.

The Hearnden family lived at Blandry Farm, Acrise, and with six children to support, Caroline Hearnden lived right on the poverty line. When offered the opportunity to acquire a little extra money to help make ends meet, she agreed to Mrs Marsh's idea and just before Christmas 1883 her ten-year-old daughter Elizabeth went into the service of Miss Johnson.

In an act that now seems rather callous, but was apparently common in those harder times, Mrs Hearnden made no effort to contact her daughter for the next three months. However, she assumed all was well until Annie Johnson turned up on her doorstep on 8 March 1884 complaining that the child had developed some disgusting habits and lacked manners. She then asked for a sheet of paper and wrote down several lines of script before asking Mrs Hearnden to sign it to say she was in agreement with what was written down. The poor woman, not wishing to show that she could neither read or write, pretended to read it and then made a cross for a signature, unaware that she had just agreed for her daughter to be sent away on the pretext she was to be trained by Sisters of Mercy for use as a domestic servant. In reality, Miss Johnson, after deducing that Caroline Hearnden didn't care because of her lack of contact with her daughter, was now prepared to sell the girl on.

However, she was wrong. After a sleepless night when the thought of what she may have actually signed away preyed on her mind, Mrs Hearnden travelled to Folkestone and asked Annie Johnson if she could see her daughter. She was told that this was not possible because she had signed a piece of paper agreeing for the girl to be sent away to London and if she caused a disturbance her daughter would never be seen again. During a further visit on 18 March Mrs Hearnden was told that her daughter had been taken away by a Sister Mary and if they met up at the *Black Bull* public house the next day they could travel up to London to see her. Temporarily reassured, Mrs Hearnden arrived at the pub at the appointed time, but after it became obvious Miss Johnson was not going to turn up, she went to inform the police of her missing child.

Miss Johnson was promptly taken into custody under suspicion

The site of Annie Johnson's boarding house, pictured shortly before the properties were demolished. Marlinova Collection

"Black Bull"
. Hotel, .

Canterbury Rd.,
FOLKESTONE.

Five minutes' walk
from Junction Station.

Proprietor :
T. E. POWELL.

Bowling Green
and Tea Gardens.

Noted for Wines and
Spirits, Ales, Cigars,
ETC.

Parties Catered for

W. ANDERSON,
Manager.

BY]   [NEAME, FOLKESTONE.

The *Black Bull* Hotel, Folkestone, where Annie Johnson was due to meet Caroline Hearnden but failed to turn up. Alan F. Taylor

of unlawfully taking a child away from its mother, and further enquires revealed that she had previously been suspected of the same offence. In May 1883 a woman named Buckland had complained that her seventeen-year-old daughter had disappeared from the same lodging house. The police enquires into that case had come to a dead end, but the girl was later discovered to be living in Plumstead.

Rumours quickly spread around the town that Miss Johnson had murdered young Eliza Hearnden, and as a result, a great deal of ill-feeling was directed against her. A large and vociferous crowd gathered outside the house while the police was searching it and several windows were smashed by stones. Later all her goods and furniture were seized and sold. The local newspaper, the *Folkestone Chronicle*, also got in on the act by commenting (on 26 April 1884):

> *Every day the mystery with regard to the missing child deepens. A man informed some servants that he saw the child only a couple of days before she was missed. She looked much emaciated, and her knuckles showed signs of bad treatment. My theory is that the*

child's remains are yet to be found in, or near, Folkestone. The
house ought to be searched from cellar to garret, planks taken up and
all wells or cesspools etc fully explored. A stigma rests upon this
'Queen of Watering Places' and the sooner it is removed the sweeter
will the town smell.

Annie Johnson was duly charged with the offence for which she
had been arrested, but her trial had to be postponed twice while
the police made a thorough search for the missing girl. The
accused led the police a merry dance after telling them the girl
may have gone to a Sisters of Mercy home in Finchley, which
proved not to be the case, whilst a railway porter told them Miss
Johnson had told him that the girl had gone to St Joseph's in
Folkestone; a thorough search also proved that to be a lie. Over
6,000 handbills were distributed at home and abroad; however,
nothing more was ever heard of the missing girl.

Eventually the defendant did appear before the local magistrates at Folkestone Town Hall, where the attorney for the
prosecution quashed rumours that the child had been murdered,
but said he had been instructed the child was being detained
somewhere by persons in collusion with the defendant. The
strong local feeling against Miss Johnson remained in evidence
throughout the proceedings when she was constantly shouted and
barracked at, and the bench at times had difficulty keeping order.
The jury, after some deliberation, decided that the case should be
referred to the Central Criminal Court in London because of the
strong local prejudice, and the date was fixed for 19 May 1884.

Yet, in spite of a spirited defence by her lawyers, the continuing
stonewalling by Annie Johnson on where the missing child was,
along with her many previous lies, ensured that a Guilty verdict
was recorded and a sentence of twelve months hard labour
handed out.

The disappearance of Elizabeth Hearnden, and her ultimate
fate, remained a popular topic of discussion in Folkestone for
many years. All manner of theories were advanced on what had
happened to her; the most popular being that she had been sent
across to the continent, where she may have come to no good.
Others thought she had been murdered and disposed off by Annie
Johnson before she went to see Mrs Hearnden for the first time.
Sadly, we shall never know.

CHAPTER 13

The Scourge of the Demon Drink

Sandgate, 1888

Poor Fanny Hancock ended her days chained-up in an asylum cell deranged with a madness that had been heightened by her fondness for alcohol, the 'scourge of the demon drink'. In those days before the caring society and social workers her frequent attempts at suicide and cruelty to her children when under the influence of drink had been sadly left unchecked, until, in the month before Jack the Ripper began his own series of heinous crimes, Fanny was to commit her own 'Orrible Murder'.

Fanny Hancock's drinking affected everyone she was close to. Her husband had seen her descend into the abyss during her transformation from a sweet, pretty girl into a demonic Jekyll-and-Hyde character who usually took out her frequent drunken rages on him. For ten years he put up with it and suffered until he could take it no more. In early 1886 he fled to Bath, leaving behind his ten-year-old daughter to cope with her mother's increasingly erratic behaviour.

With her husband out of the way, Fanny took up with a man named William Williams and he was soon to find out to his cost what he had taken on. In June 1886 Williams found himself in court charged with assaulting Fanny at the Bouverie Laundry, where he worked. It appears that Fanny had turned up at the laundry on the pretext of visiting her sister, who also worked there, but she really came to confront and berate Williams. The case was dismissed, yet Fanny was to reappear in court later that same day charged with attempting to commit suicide by jumping off the harbour pier. Two labourers had witnessed her in the act and dragged her away before she could accomplish it. On both occasions Fanny had been worse for drink and had become violent and suicidal as a result.

Yet Williams stuck with Fanny and they moved into lodgings at 102 Foord Road, Folkestone, where a baby was born to the couple. However, within a few months of the baby's birth Fanny

Baby-killer Fanny Hancock spent some time living in Foord Road, which ran beneath Folkestone's towering Foord Viaduct. Marlinova Collection

was up before the magistrates again, this time charged with holding her baby down in a pail of water, and was bound over. The hapless family of four then moved into 126 Guildhall Street and became five in March 1888 when Fanny gave birth to a baby girl. All the while, Fanny's mental state continued to deteriorate and in May 1888 her longsuffering eldest daughter ran to the police and reported that her mother had walked into the sea. A full search of the area was undertaken for what was expected to be a dead body, yet Fanny surprised everyone by reappearing in Sandgate the next day drunkenly abusing anyone who happened to pass by her prostrate form.

And it was to Sandgate that she would return for her final, and ultimately tragic, act. After a hard day's drinking in the *Alexandra Hotel* she was spotted walking up and down the beach with her young son and the babe-in-arms by two patients from the Beach Rocks convalescent home, Benjamin Pain and Richard Cottingham. Their jolly banter about the woman's drunken misdemeanour was stopped suddenly when she was seen rushing headlong into the sea carrying and dragging her children with her. The two men rushed to the rescue and managed to drag Fanny and her son alive out of the water but the baby was nowhere to be seen, although the shawl she was wrapped in was recovered.

The police were called from the nearby station at Seabrook. They thought Fanny was exhibiting 'peculiar symptoms' and sent her to the hospital in Dover Road, Folkestone. The boy, meanwhile, was taken into the care of a shoemaker named Cottage, who lived in Devonshire Terrace, opposite the beach.

Under questioning at the hospital, Fanny stated at first she had purposely drowned the baby, but then retracted her confession and said she had followed the boy, who had run into the sea. They were all knocked over by a large wave, which had knocked the baby out of her arms. Sadly, on the day after the tragedy, two men named William Rogers and George Climpson, who were lodging at 1 Earls Avenue, Folkestone, found the baby's body on the beach near the tollhouse on the Lower Sandgate Road.

126 Guildhall Street, Folkestone (until recently Guildhall Autos) was where the baby murdered by Fanny Hancock was born. Marlinova Collection

Fanny Hancock drowned her baby daughter on the beach close to Devonshire Terrace, Sandgate. Marlinova Collection

At the coroner's inquest, the pitiful state of the baby at the time of her death was wretchedly revealed to all. As well as being severely undernourished (the poor child weighed only seven pounds, as opposed to the fourteen to sixteen pounds she should have weighed for a child of her age), she was found to be clothed in a few pitiful rags that were tied to her body with a bit of string. Perhaps swayed by the evidence that Fanny had often threatened to drown herself and her children, the jury found her guilty of drowning her baby. She was then brought before Folkestone Magistrates, where a Guilty verdict was also recorded. At both hearings Fanny sat quietly in the dock, resolutely refusing to give any evidence.

The case was ordered to be brought before the County Assizes at Maidstone, where Fanny pleaded guilty. Before a packed court, she decided this time to give a good exhibition of her peculiar behaviour and fended off every question with either positive or negative expletives. She resolutely refused to say anything else, which hardly helped her cause. The jury duly returned a Guilty verdict and she was sentenced to death. However, it was obvious she was insane and the sentence was later commuted to life internment inside the County Asylum.

The eldest daughter and the son were found new homes, while William Williams sloped off to pastures new. As Fanny lay incarcerated in her tiny cell, only she knew the truth of what had really happened to her baby daughter.

CHAPTER 14

A 'Jack the Ripper' Suspect

Elham and Folkestone, 1888

The unsolved 'Jack the Ripper' murders of 1888 spread their panic and fear far outside the confines of the East End of London. Anyone found with blood on their hands during that Autumn of Terror became an immediate suspect; including a down-and-out vagrant who turned up at the Elham Union Workhouse just outside Folkestone. Furthermore, Folkestone itself was to earn a place in the annals of this most notorious of murders when one of the infamous 'Jack the Ripper' letters was sent from the town.

On 7 August 1888 the body of Martha Tabram was found in George Yard Buildings, Whitechapel; and so began the reign of the Whitechapel Murderer, now known as Jack the Ripper. Martha, a 39-year-old prostitute, had been stabbed no less than thirty-nine times. In a crime-ridden East End of London, the murder was soon yesterday's news until, on 31 August, another prostitute was the victim of an even more frenzied attack. Polly Nicholls was discovered at 3.40 a.m. in Buck's Row with a badly mutilated throat and severe stab wounds to the stomach and abdomen. Polly had earlier been turned away from her lodging house because she did not have the 4d doss money, and as she walked away, cheerfully called out, 'I'll soon get my doss money!' and 'See what a jolly bonnet I've got now!'

The murder of Polly Nicholls was soon linked to that of Martha Tabram, and also to the earlier slaying of Emma Elizabeth Smith on 3 April (despite Emma clearly stating before she died that a gang had been responsible for the attack on her). Nevertheless, it was not until the murder of Annie Chapman on 8 September that the East End realised that it had a knife-wielding maniac in its midst. Forty-seven-year-old Annie had been found in the rear yard of 29 Hanbury Street with appalling mutilations to her body. These included a deep cut to the throat (almost severing it from the body), and the abdomen ripped open to remove the stomach and small intestine, which were placed beside the body. The murderer had taken the uterus away with him.

Panic now raced through the East End and began to spread beyond, throughout the country. The inability of the police to apprehend the killer led to vigilante groups being formed, who homed in on anyone who had blood on their hands or remotely resembled what the murderer was supposed to have looked like. The prevalent feeling was that only a Jew or foreigner was capable of committing such a heinous series of crimes, and therefore anti-Semitic feeling was at fever pitch. This led to the arrest of a Polish Jew named John Pizer; a bootmaker known to all as 'Leather Apron'. Pizer had a history of violence to women, but his cast-iron alibi proved he could not have been the killer.

Outside the East End, other possible 'suspects' were being targeted. They included William Piggott, who had been arrested in a Gravesend pub shouting out his hatred of women. When it was discovered he had a cut hand and a parcel containing a bloody shirt, he was hailed as the Whitechapel Murderer. However, it was soon proved that Piggott was completely innocent and so he was let go.

The Whitechapel Murders were now touching every corner of the country and Annie Chapman's death was the first to be reported in the Folkestone newspapers. Everyone awaited the murderer's next move, and on 30 September 1888 he duly struck again, with the 'Double Event'. At around 1 a.m. the body of Elizabeth Stride was discovered in Dutfield's Yard, Berner Street. However, unlike the previous victims, 'Long Liz' had suffered only a cut throat, and it appears that the murderer was disturbed in his work by Louis Diemschutz driving his cart into the yard. With his bloodlust seemingly unsatisfied, the murderer made his way towards the City and came across Kate Eddowes. Cheerful Kate had just been released from Bishopsgate Police Station after being detained for drunkenness, but in a dark corner of Mitre Square her life was literally ripped out of her. In addition to the usual deep throat cut, the face had been mutilated and the abdomen ripped open to allow the contents to spill over the body. A kidney was missing, which presumably the killer took away with him (a portion of 'ginny kidney' was later sent to George Lusk, Chairman of the Mile End Vigilance Committee).

The killer must have made his escape north-east through the district, as part of Kate's bloodstained apron (which the killer had used to clean his knife) was found at the entrance to 108–119 Wentworth Model Dwellings, Goulston Street. Inside the building, chalked on a wall, was the message, 'The Juwes are The

Men That will Not Be Blamed for Nothing'. Whether this was written by the murderer will never be known, and it was quickly cleaned off for fear of inspiring anti-Semitic riots.

The Double Event left not only the East End of London cowering in fear, but the country as a whole. A letter received by the police from someone claiming he was the murderer (but probably a hoax) had been signed off by 'Jack the Ripper' and from now on this would be his infamous sobriquet. Nationwide, would-be Jacks were being apprehended on the flimsiest of pretexts and south-east Kent had its own pretender. On 13 October 1888 the *Folkestone Express* reported:

What may turn out to be an important arrest has been made at Elham, in the detention of a casual who has come to the workhouse under the most suspicious of circumstances.

It would appear that on Monday [8 October] *Mr Kingsmill, the Relieving Officer, observed a man walking along the road towards the Union, whose appearance aroused his suspicions, and he called the attention of the Master of the Union to the circumstance, should the man apply for admission. The man came to the Union and applied for the shelter of the casual ward, and Mr Young was so struck with his resemblance to the portrait and description of the man wanted, published in the* Daily Telegraph, *that his suspicions were immediately aroused. The man is about 23–25 years of age, dressed in the shabby genteel style, black cloth coat, check pattern waistcoat and hard brown felt hat. Observing his clothes, Mr Young saw what he thought to be smears of blood on his trousers and shirt. The cuffs of his shirt had evidently been cut or ripped off. On his person was found a pocket-handkerchief and a piece of sponge. His manner was nervous and uneasy. He said at first he wanted to come into the house as an inmate for a few weeks. On Tuesday, however, he wanted to go away, but Mr Young thought the affair so suspicious he detained him. The detained man further excited suspicion by the contradictory account of himself, which he has furnished. He first said he was named Wilson, and has given 3 or 4 other different names. He stated he came from Camberwell, and was a plumber's labourer and had walked to the Union from Dover. But as he has made several contradictory statements, no reliance could be placed on what he said. To the Guardian, who saw him on Thursday, he said his name was McCarthy. Superintendent Maxted was communicated with, and he has made investigations into the matter, the man being detained under his care. The London Police have been communicated with.*

In the following week, the *Folkestone Chronicle* carried a report on the Elham suspect. This is of interest for its comments on local people's reactions, and the hundreds of 'Jack the Ripper' suspect scares the police had to deal with:

THE CAPTURE AT ELHAM

A tramp was detained at Elham Union last week on suspicion of being concerned in the Whitechapel Tragedies, but the 'arrest' turns out to be as important as a great many previous scares. The suspicions were aroused by one of the relieving officers who had first noticed him on the road to the workhouse. Upon arriving at the house, he asked to be allowed to enter the Hospital for a week or two, as he was unwell. He suffered from a weak heart, and desired to see the doctor. The man appears to have undergone a most minute examination by the relieving officer and the master. He was compared with the sketches of the 'supposed' murderer, which appeared in the Daily Telegraph *a short time ago, and pronounced to bear a striking resemblance, although the police state that they failed to detect any likeness, except about the forehead. Some marks of blood were said to have been seen by the Master on the trousers and shirt, but when officially examined by the police, it was left an open question, as the smears were indistinct. Although the Workhouse officials felt so certain that they were detaining the actual murderer, no communications were made to the police until the third day, and then to Scotland Yard, without mentioning a single word to the County Police, notwithstanding that Supt. Maxted's office was but a few miles distant. Upon receipt of the message the officials at Scotland Yard immediately communicated with Supt. Maxted, requesting him to investigate this case. Accordingly he visited the Union, and, after examining the man, states that he is fully convinced that he has no connection whatever with the crime for which he was detained. In answer to the officer's questions he stated that he was discharged from the 16th Lancers at Dublin on the 8th of August 1888 and produced his discharge, which showed he was 'discharged as unfit for further service'. He arrived in London soon after his discharge, and tried to get work, but was unable to do so. He admitted that he gave a false name when he entered the Workhouse, and he was very sorry he had done so. His name was not George Wilson, but John Jeffrey, by which name he was known in the Army. Some time after his confession, Supt. Maxted requested him to write his name, which he unhesitatingly wrote as 'George William McCarthy, 23 years of age', and confessed that this was his actual name. He was the son of Mr James McCarthy, a civil engineer, of Ivanhoe Road, Denmark Park, Camberwell, but he appeared confused and loath to answer questions touching upon family affairs. The officer did not acquaint him with the fact that he was detained on suspicion of being concerned in the Whitechapel Murders, but in the course of 'ordinary' conversation he stated that he slept at a lodging house in Red Cross Court for several nights, whilst attempting to find work. The opinion there, he said, was 'that the murderer was either a medical man or a mad butcher'. He slept at the same house on the night of the last two murders, but on the next morning left and proceeded to Hounslow, where he attempted to enlist in the Royal Fusilier Militia. He saw Sergt-Major Cutbush, but as he afterwards expressed a desire to enter a cavalry regiment he was requested to proceed to Canterbury and told his papers would follow. He accordingly went to Canterbury, and slept there on Thursday night. He left the barracks on Friday and walked on to Dover, where he stayed until Monday, sleeping at the Union, and on one evening (Saturday) at Philip's lodging-house. On Monday he proceeded to Elham, and ultimately to the workhouse at Eachend-hill. Supt. Maxted instructed Sergt. Hoad to make enquires at Philip's lodging house, Dover, as to whether this statement was correct. The landlord bore out the statement, adding that the man was very quiet in his manner, and retired to bed very early. The statement as to his whereabouts since leaving Dublin has been found to be correct. He was examined on Friday by Dr Bishop, who found that his heart was quite unaffected, but he will be detained a few days, in order that another examination may be made as to the state of his mind. Supt. Maxted states that the man's height is 5ft. 7 1/2 inches, he is of medium build, has dark brown hair, brown eyes, a slight moustache, and of superior appearance, he was dressed in a black coat and trousers (very torn), brown vest, with a brown, hard felt hat, and a pair of boots having several cuts across the uppers, presumably for the purpose of comfort in walking.*

THE ARREST AT ELHAM

The force of imagination under something like panic never had a better illustration than in the case of the detention of a young man at Elham Union. As soon as the Guardians separated, those who represented rural parts, carried the news to their homes that a man was in the Union who might turn out to be the Whitechapel Murderer. They were questioned, cross-examined, re-examined, and every word on the subject readily listened to, and they simply gave an account of what had transpired at the Union. At Lyminge in the afternoon, it was confidently stated that 'Jack the Ripper' had been caught with the terrible instrument in his possession, and all traces of his recent bloodthirsty exploits found upon his person, whilst one individual, the possessor of a highly strung imagination, averred that the reward for his detention was on its way from London, and would equally be divided between the two gentlemen responsible for his detention. At Lympne, at Postling, and wherever the news travelled, reports of all kinds spread like wildfire, and one party expressed a determination to walk to the Union, if by chance they might get a sight of such a distinguished character. At Elham, as in other places, extreme gratification was expressed amongst the ladies, one formidable damsel remarking that she now 'could now walk about of a night time without having the creeps come over her'. Children were heard with gleeful satisfaction shouting 'we've caught Jack the Ripper.' The thought naturally suggests itself that if in these rural parts rumours of such an exaggerated character could arise out of simple circumstance – namely, the detention of a man for a few days to elucidate certain mysterious appearances – what trouble the police of London must have had in enquiring into the hundreds of reported suspicious cases which they daily receive from all parts of the country. Enquiry soon elicited that this man, who in the contradictory accounts he gave of himself, is responsible for the

The old Elham Union Workhouse, where a man was detained on suspicion of being Jack the Ripper. Marlinova Collection

An inmate of the Elham Union Workhouse undertaking menial tasks to pay for his upkeep. Marlinova Collection

unenviable notoriety he has gained – was free from any association with the crime, and the joy with which the report that the Whitechapel murderer had been caught, will be succeeded by the credulous people who believed the rumour with that disappointment arising from the contradiction of news 'too good to be true'.

So George McCarthy's brief notoriety as 'Jack the Ripper' was over and he wandered off back to obscurity. The police, quite rightly, quickly established that he had nothing to do with the murders, but at least the furore had brought some of the excitement and hysteria of the crimes down to a quiet corner of rural Kent. The children of Elham could no longer chant that they had caught Jack the Ripper, but they made up for it by supplanting Guy Fawkes with Jack on their 5 November bonfires.

Meanwhile, the real murderer had lain silent since the Double Event and it began to be assumed that the whole ghastly nightmare might be at an end. Then, on the morning of 9 November, Jack struck with his most savage killing yet. Inside 13 Millers Court, Dorset Street, the occupant Mary Jane (or Marie Jeanette) Kelly had been slaughtered and dismembered as if she was an animal carcass. A pretty redhead of about twenty-five, Kelly's face had been hacked beyond recognition (which leaves a slight doubt if it was actually her?). In addition, her breasts had been cut off and the abdomen ripped open so that the uterus, liver, kidney and intestines could be placed by the body and on the bedside table. The heart was missing.

A few days after the murder, a postcard dated 11 November 1888 was sent to 'Mrs McCarthy, No. 28 Dorset Street, London, East End'. It read:

From Jack ['Sheridan' deleted]
The ripper
Folkestone
Nov 11 1888

Dear Boss I am getting lively on the move baint I made a good job last time getting better each time a good joke I played on them three ladies one ['death' smudged out] *Died two frighened* [sic] *Next time a woman and her Daughter ta ta.*
Dear Boss [drawing of a man with a knife or axe over a victim followed by a P and another man with a knife. In the corner is a cage with a figure inside].

The postcard was pre-printed on the correspondence side with 'From' 'Folkestone' and '188'. The address side had a halfpenny red stamp with a Folkestone postmark and the date 'Nov 11 1888' (the postal service at that time was excellent and local mail was often received the same day it was posted).

The Mrs McCarthy mentioned on the postcard was the wife of John McCarthy, the landlord of Mary Kelly's room at 13 Millers Court as well as other rooms in Dorset Street. Collectively the rooms were known as 'McCarthy's Rents.' McCarthy, who was a 37-year-old naturalised British subject (having been born in France), also held a chandler's shop at 27 Dorset Street. On the morning of Friday, 9 November 1888 he had sent his odd-job man Thomas Bowyer to collect the rent money (which was weeks in arrears) from Kelly. After receiving no answer from his knock at the door, Bowyer put his hand through a broken window and pulled back the curtain. What he saw sent him racing off to fetch McCarthy, who, after taking a peep at the carnage inside the room, set off as fast as his legs could carry him to Commercial Road Police Station. A number of policemen, including Inspector Beck, accompanied him back to Millers Court, but no further action was taken for several hours because bloodhounds were expected on the scene. When they failed to arrive, McCarthy

The 'Jack the Ripper' postcard sent to Mrs McCarthy (landlady of final victim Mary Kelly) from Folkestone.
Marlinova Collection

broke down the door to the room with an axe handle on the orders of Inspector Arnold.

McCarthy was understandably in a state of shock for some time after the murder, and to compound his woes a number of his tenants fled their rooms in fear. It is said he had a great fondness for Kelly, which explains why he allowed her to run up arrears on her rent (unlike his other tenants) and was buried close to her last resting-place in Leytonstone Roman Catholic cemetery.

The postcard, which was almost certainly a hoax, was probably acquired and written in Folkestone by a traveller on his way to the continent aboard the Channel steamers. A thorough search of the Kelly's directories for the Folkestone area between the years 1885 and 1895 has failed to reveal a single person called Sheridan, although it is extremely unlikely anyone would have been stupid enough to use their real name! It is not certain whether Scotland Yard ever followed up the postcard but, along with the majority of the Ripper correspondence, they appeared not to have taken it too seriously. The postcard received no mention at all in the Folkestone newspapers, although they may have been unaware of its existence.

The sending of the postcard to the shell-shocked McCarthys was obviously intended for maximum effect, and the rather sick individual delighted in using the stock Ripper letter words 'Dear Boss', 'job', 'joke' and of course 'Jack the Ripper'. These had been a feature of the 'Dear Boss' letter sent to the Central News Agency on 25 September 1888, which coined the 'Jack the Ripper' name. Curiously, of course, McCarthy was also the name of the vagrant arrested at the local workhouse on suspicion of being Jack the Ripper.

In its edition of the 24 November 1888 the *Folkestone Chronicle* could not resist sensationalising the Elham suspect one last time, and bemoaning Scotland Yard's lack of interest in him:

THE WHITECHAPEL MURDERS – THE SUSPECTED MAN AT ELHAM WORKHOUSE

The fact that the Scotland Yard authorities took no pains to verify the statements and the identity of the tramp who was recently detained at the Elham Union Workhouse has caused some surprise to the authorities there. It will be remembered that the front of the man's trousers had been soaked in blood, that there were blood spatters on his shirt front, and that his shirt wristbands had been recently torn off. By his own showing, he was familiar with the low

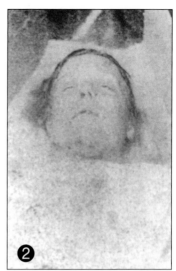

The six victims of Jack the Ripper:
1 Martha Tabram,
2 Polly Nicholls
3 Annie Chapman
4 Liz Stride
5 Kate Eddowes (2)
6 Mary Kelly (2).
Marlinova Collection

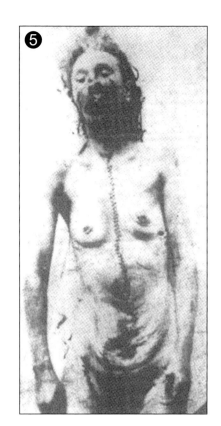

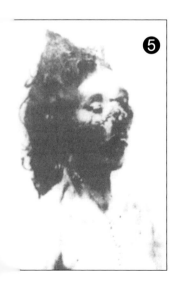

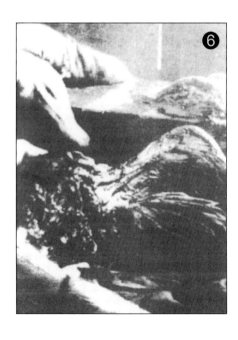

lodging houses at the East End of London, and has been staying in one in the Borough for some period until he started, as he said, on the night when the murders in Berners Street [sic] and Mitre Square were committed, for the country. The authorities at the Union detained him for as long as they could on one pretext or another and at length allowed him to depart, about ten days before the woman Kelly was killed. Prior to the man's departure, Dr Bishop, the medical officer of the Union, examined the man's clothing somewhat minutely, and found traces of bloody finger marks in both his pockets. The man's shirtsleeves, beyond where the wristbands had been, were also splattered with blood. He was seen afterwards on the road, carrying a paper parcel. His dress and appearance answer pretty accurately to one of the descriptions in the daily papers of a man said to have been in Kelly's company on the night of the murder.

However, George McCarthy was clearly not Jack the Ripper, and with the Kelly murder it seems likely the real culprit had finished his work. Scotland Yard closed the case in 1892, but the theories on the identity of this most notorious and mysterious of killers will forever rage on.

CHAPTER 15

A Surfeit of Young Bodies

Folkestone, Seabrook and Sellindge
1867–1922

*Modern methods of contraception, and if that has failed, termina-
tion, have virtually eliminated the dilemma of an unwanted baby.
Unfortunately, in the not-too-distant past you had little choice if
you were pregnant but to go through with it. For an unmarried
mother, there was a great shame and stigma in having a child out
of wedlock, which would often lead to an extended stay in a workhouse or even an asylum. Some, however, were prepared to resort to
other means to spare themselves this humiliation.*

On the morning of Sunday, 14 July 1867 Albert Brown, a
miller at Bradstone Mill, Folkestone, was quietly
walking his dog by the mill when to his horror he
discovered the badly decomposed body of a newborn
male child lying in the millpond close to the viaduct. An examination of the child found five to six inches of umbilical cord still
attached, which showed it had not been properly attended to at
birth. A piece of line had been tied around the neck and outside
the knot the line was in a noose, indicating a stone had been used
to weigh the body down. The mother was never found, and it
could not be proved whether the baby had been stillborn or was
murdered soon after birth.

An unusual and rather horrible case of child murder was
reported in the *Folkestone Chronicle* of 2 January 1886:

*An inquest was held at Sellindge on Tuesday, 21 December 1885
on the body of a male child, unknown, apparently about four or
five months old. From the evidence it appeared that the child had
either been thrown onto the railway or had been thrown from the
train, on Christmas Day, most probably from the train. The jury
reached a verdict of 'wilful murder against some person or persons
unknown'.*

In the following week the paper followed up the report with:

One of Folkestone's grisly baby parcels was found in the shadow of the Foord
Viaduct in 1867. Marlinova Collection

> *The police have been actively engaged during the week in the*
> *endeavour to discover the perpetrator of the murder of the male*
> *infant whose body was found between Ashford and Westenhanger*
> *Junction (at Sellindge). The child, it appears, was between seven*
> *and eight months old, and the police are enabled to say conclusively*
> *that it was brought from Dover on the up train which left at 1.55*
> *a.m. on Christmas Day. It is believed that a person who got alone*
> *into a first-class compartment with a Gladstone bag was the party*
> *who had the child. According to the testimony of Dr Charlton, who*
> *examined the body, the little thing had been nearly starved to death,*
> *but he believes that it was thrown out of the window alive.*

Sadly the perpetrator of this terrible deed was never traced, and
no more was reported of the case.

On the afternoon of 26 March 1890 the Commanding Officer
of the Royal Engineers at Shorncliffe Camp, Colonel Bell VC, was
expecting a total of ten packages to be brought to him from
Sandgate railway station. However, the driver sent to fetch the
parcels became puzzled by the fact that there were eleven packages addressed to the Colonel. The additional artefact, it seems,

was a large two-gallon stone pickle jar. Nevertheless, it was loaded onto the cart with the others and the driver began making his way back up to the camp.

Unfortunately, the driver's horse made heavy weather of the steep ascent of Hospital Hill with its heavy load. A wheel became jammed in a hole in the road, causing the cart to jolt and the bung to come flying off the pickle jar. Upon retrieving the bung, the driver noticed, to his horror, two feet sticking out of the jar, and ran down the hill as fast as his legs could carry him to report his grisly find to the police officers on duty at Seabrook.

When the body was hauled out of the jar, it was found to be a newborn male infant bearing several marks of violence. The origin of the jar was eventually traced by Scotland Yard to the South Eastern Railway House in Regent Street, and from there to an aristocratic young lady in the heart of the fashionable West End of London. However, during questioning by the police she managed to persuade them the squeamish contents of the jar were formerly the property of her brother: a doctor and keen keeper of human specimens who had passed away four years previously. Incredibly, the police decided to accept this explanation and dropped their investigation; much to the chagrin of some, who felt the wealth and status of the young lady had enabled her to get away with a hideous crime.

If the lady was innocent, why were there marks of violence on the body? Furthermore, what had Colonel Bell done to deserve such a gruesome parcel?

Just over three years later, on the bright morning of Wednesday, 23 July 1893, William John Ratcliff was passing Christ Church in Sandgate Road, Folkestone, when he noticed a brown-paper parcel tied with string in the area of the north transept. After inquisitively inspecting the bundle he decided to open it, but upon breaking the string the feet of a baby child sprang out.

Leaving the body in a toolshed, Ratcliff ran off to fetch the police and was accompanied back to the church by Sergeant Butcher. When the policeman opened the remainder of the parcel the body was seen to be wrapped in two layers of petticoats, a chemise and a piece of glazed pink cambric that had come from a dressing table. The poor baby had apparently been suffocated by having a diaper thrust into its mouth and tape tightly knotted around its neck. This was confirmed by Marcus Bateman, the surgeon who examined the body, who thought the baby was two or three days old at the time of its death.

The jury at the coroner's inquest returned a verdict of wilful murder against some persons unknown, but due to the lack of evidence the case was not followed up, in spite of a clue being found on the body. This was a bill stamped 'Cash Stores, Ashford' for some articles manufactured by H. Morrell of Rye, yet it failed to stir the police into action. Local rumour had it that the murderer may have been a maid engaged in the service of the one of the prominent families of Folkestone's West End, who had been impregnated by the master of the house and killed the baby to avoid shaming herself.

Someone had got away with murder; and twelve years later, on Sunday, 20 June 1905, in an almost identical case, the act was repeated by another newborn-baby killer.

The early-morning walk to church by three housemaids was suddenly stopped when they saw a parcel in the churchyard of Folkestone Parish Church near the wall of West Cliff Gardens. Perhaps having heard of other gruesome encounters of parcels left in churchyards, the ladies did not attempt to inspect it too closely and went for help. Upon examination, the parcel was found to contain the body of a newborn baby and it was later established that the child had been suffocated within a few hours of its birth.

Nevertheless, although it was evident that a criminal act had

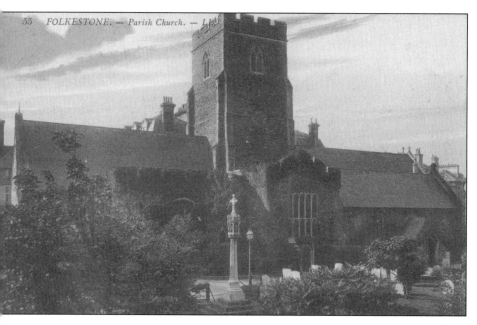

Folkestone's Parish Church of St Mary and St Eanswythe, where the body of a newborn baby was discovered in 1905. Marlinova Collection

been committed, the case was not followed up and a convenient snuffing-out of an unwanted life had been allowed to pass.

The year 1917 in Folkestone will always be remembered for the terrible air raid on 25 May that killed seventy-two townsfolk; however, there was also horror of a different kind with the finding of two more baby parcels.

On 4 January 1917, Sidney Moore, the relief clerk at Folkestone Junction station, received a package off the 4.03 p.m. train from London marked 'Miss S. Moore (was this just a co-incidence of names?), Swingfield, near Dover, Kent – to be left until called for.' A parcel label was also attached marked 'S.E. & C.R. Chislehurst 1s paid', which was dated 3 January 1917 in a very faint rubber stamp. Owing to the address being outside the delivery zone, the receipt for the parcel was sent to the Swingfield address on both 5 and 20 January, but it remained uncollected. Eventually, the parcel began to emit an unpleasant odour that led to the police to be called on 15 February. D.S. Johnson was given the thankless task of opening the parcel and, to his horror, found the body of a male infant covered in blood from a fractured skull.

The elusive Miss S. Moore of Swingfield was never traced (did she ever exist, or was someone playing a very sick practical joke on Sidney Moore?) and all police enquires in Chislehurst turned up nothing.

However, Miss Mary Ann Miles was not so fortunate: her infanticidal crime was discovered and she duly appeared before the Folkestone Police Court on Tuesday, 11 December 1917 charged with concealing the birth of her child.

Miss Miles had spent a fortnight in October 1917 at the lodging house of Mrs Simmons at 58 Coolinge Road, Folkestone, but had left in rather a hurry, taking, it appeared, the blanket from her bed. Around a month later, Mrs Simmons was cleaning out the box room at the top of the house when, to her shock, she discovered the missing blanket wrapped around the badly decomposed body of a male infant. All suspicions immediately pointed to Miss Miles, who was traced working at the New Era Laundry in Cheriton. Under questioning she admitted suffocating her newborn baby and was committed for trial at the Kent Assizes at Maidstone. In court, the judge appeared to take pity on the unfortunate girl, who had obviously failed to take great steps to conceal her crime or to take flight from the area, and she was committed to an asylum.

The finding of two further baby parcels in 1920 led to Folkestone gaining the unfortunate distinction of 'Infanticide Capital of Kent'. The first case occurred in February, when

51. FOLKESTONE (Angleterre). - Ville, Port de Mer, de 23.700 habitants

Belle vue du haut des falaises. A vu naître, en 1578, Thomas Hervey,
qui découvrit la circulation du sang.

In 1917 Miss Mary Anne Miles hid the body of her baby in the box room at
No. 58 Coolinge Road, Folkestone. Alan F. Taylor

gravedigger Henry Jarvis found a brown-paper parcel by the main
wall of the cemetery fronting Cheriton Road. When he un-
wrapped the paper, the body of a young infant was discovered,
who was duly found to have been suffocated.

In the following August the corpse of another infant was
discovered, but this time in quite bizarre circumstances. At
around 6 a.m. on the morning of Friday, 13 August, Frederick
Luck, a gardener, was on his way to work at the Wear Bay
Gardens when he noticed a brown canvas bag lying on the
pathway at the junction of Wear Bay Crescent and Warren Road
on Folkestone's East Cliff. On finding the bag heavy to lift and
perhaps anticipating something of value inside, he took it to his
tool house at the gardens and then home with him at breakfast.
However, by this time, the bag had begun to emit a particularly
nasty smell and it was decided to call the police. PC Cox arrived

at the house at 4 Penfold Road, but found he was unable to open the bag, so he slit open the side with a knife. The origin of the smell was found to be the body of a male infant wrapped in a piece of counterpane. The coroner later reported that a blow to the head had probably killed the baby, although, as in nearly all similar cases, it would prove impossible to find those responsible.

The final case, in 1922, once again involved a railway station and was thought to have been the result of an accidental death rather than murder.

On Friday, 29 September, at 7.00 a.m., Miss Ethel Hope, a buffet attendant at Folkestone Central station, noticed a newspaper parcel under the seat of the ladies' lavatory on the up platform. Upon moving it she noticed that the parcel was heavy and felt cold, and thought it best to report what she had found to her manager. Yet it appears nothing further was done until the following morning when May Sergeant, the ladies' waiting-room attendant, decided to report the matter directly to the police.

Upon his arrival at the station, Police Inspector James Burrows initially thought the parcel contained fish, but soon changed his mind on discovering the head of a child when he pulled back the paper. The perpetrators of this deed proved themselves to have

The body of a young child was found in the ladies' lavatory at Folkestone Central station in 1922. Marlinova Collection

had a rather sick sense of humour by wrapping the tiny body in a copy of the *News of the World* with the headline, 'Baby Found in a Parcel'.

Nevertheless, the coroner thought the baby had died following an accidental fall to the head and recorded a verdict of accidental death.

Thankfully, thereafter, the rather too numerous cases of Folkestone 'Baby Parcels' petered out (although an infant's body was discovered on the beach in 1925) and the town could finally shake off its embarrassing 'Infanticide Capital of Kent' title.

CHAPTER 16

The Baby Farmer

Folkestone, 1892

A peculiarity of the squalid social conditions of the late-Victorian age was the despicable practice of 'Baby Farming', where illegitimate or simply unwanted children were farmed out to women acting as foster mothers. For a price, these Baby Farmers were prepared to adopt the children or look after them for a fixed period. However, in some cases, once the money was handed over, the children were never seen or heard of again.

Harriet Mitchell of Green Street Green near Maidstone was one of these Baby Farmers, and a notorious one, to boot. She was known to have taken in numerous children from all around Kent and was suspected of ill-treating them. In some cases, the children mysteriously died within a few weeks of being placed into her care, but a lack of firm evidence meant her guilt could not be conclusively proved. Such was the case with a young Folkestone girl placed into her care.

Mrs Mitchell had been paid 4s a week by a single woman named Harriet Louise Crapnell, a waitress at a confectioner's shop in Tontine Street, to look after her little daughter Nellie. The sickly Miss Crapnell had no strong feelings for her daughter and felt that bringing her up was a struggle. Eventually, after deciding her life would be better without the burden of a young child, she handed over £10 to Mrs Mitchell to fully adopt Nellie.

However, within a few weeks of the 'adoption' having taken place, during the evening of Wednesday, 10 February 1892, a doctor was summoned to the house of Mrs Mitchell. Mitchell claimed Nellie had suffered a fit and fallen off a chair, causing her to lose consciousness. An examination by a doctor revealed that the young girl had died from her injuries, yet he felt distinctly uneasy about the circumstances surrounding her death, and said so. Furthermore, little Nellie was found to be undernourished, and dressed virtually in rags. The poor, unwanted child had simply been shunted from one unfit mother to another.

At the inquest into Nellie's death, the coroner appeared to

strongly agree with the doctor's suspicions surrounding the child's 'accident'. He scathingly commented that it was to Mrs Mitchell's advantage the child should not live after she had received the £10 to adopt it, and added that he totally abhorred the distasteful practice of Baby Farming. He ended by asking what had happened to the other missing and dead children who had been previously in the care of Mrs Mitchell.

Nevertheless, to everyone's surprise, the jury returned a verdict of accidental death and Mrs Mitchell was free to carry on with her unsavoury way of living. However, she had left the inquest with a warning from the coroner ringing in her ears that if another child died while in her care, he would make sure there would be the fullest investigation into the cause.

Tontine Street, Folkestone, where little Nellie Crapnell was sold off to a notorious 'Baby Farmer'. Marlinova Collection

FOLKESTONE. — Tontine Street. — LL.

What is now *Equilibrium* is the site of the confectioner's shop in Tontine Street where Harriet Crapnell worked as a waitress. Marlinova Collection

The despicable practice of Baby Farming was finally brought into the public eye four years later with the arrest and execution of Mrs Amelia Dyer. This 57-year-old woman is known to have killed at least seven children, but there were almost certainly others during her fifteen years as a Baby Farmer. A one-time member of the Salvation Army, Mrs Dyer moved to Reading in 1895 and began to adopt children under several aliases. Within a short time, the corpses of young children, all of them with tape around their necks, began to be fished out of the River Thames and, following police investigations, Mrs Dyer was arrested. After allegedly telling the police, 'You'll know mine by the tapes around their necks,' she admitted to the crimes and claimed they were carried out to allow her to continue to collect adoption fees for the deceased children while making room for more.

On 10 June 1896 Mrs Dyer was executed at Newgate Prison for the murder of four-month old Doris Marmon (also given up for the princely sum of £10). Her ghost thereafter was said to haunt the Chief Warder of the prison.

CHAPTER 17

Hell Hath No Fury

Folkestone, 1892

There was no getting away from it; Mary Philpott, a mariner's wife of North Street, Folkestone, and a man they just called 'Moore' positively hated each other. The cause of their long-running feud was not fully known, although many suspected it was because Mrs Philpott had once been spurned in love by Moore and had never got over it. Notwithstanding, whenever their paths crossed all hell invariably broke loose.

Matters reached a climax during the evening of Saturday, 2 April 1892. In the crowded tiny public bar of the *Royal Oak* inn in North Street on a typically boisterous Saturday night, Moore, with his dark gypsy looks and long hair, was holding court in front of a few lonely fishermen's wives. Seemingly knowing that Mrs Philpott was also in the same room (as she tended to be on most days, for drink was her only solace now), he made a particular effort to turn on the charm for his captive audience. He regaled them with stories of his life on the road, which, combined with the effects of their drinks, soon had them laughing out loud.

Mrs Philpott, on the other hand, was certainly not amused, and scowled across the bar at Moore with an evil eye. Then she snapped: one of Moore's lady acquaintances had dared touch his arm and, spotting this, Mrs Philpott stormed over to Moore and punched him hard in the mouth. He retaliated by striking her a hard blow to the face, and the two continued to strike and berate each other until a police constable was asked to intervene. Moore was sent on his way, but Mrs Philpott, who had sustained a nasty black eye and bruised forehead from the blow, continued to hang around outside the pub shouting obscenities at anyone who passed by.

On the following morning, scene two of the drama was acted out. Moore was proceeding up North Street, when he was espied by Mrs Philpott, who promptly threw some wood at him and delivered the *coup de grace* by knocking his pipe out of his mouth.

A long-vanished scene of the old fishing quarter of Folkestone where Mrs Philpott lived. Marlinova Collection

The furious Moore retaliated by pushing the woman over, causing her to strike her head on a step. Left battered and bruised for the second time in two days by a man she both loved and hated with equal passion, Mrs Philpott limped into her cottage feeling very groggy and shut the door.

To the poor, unloved fisher-wife, there seemed only one thing she could do to get even with the cad Moore: she issued a summons against him for assault. Moore promptly re-taliated with a cross-summons of his own. The two cases were heard together in Folkestone Town Hall, yet the court derisively dismissed them and both parties were ordered to pay their own costs.

Yet, despite being the cata-lyst in this whole sorry affair, a certain amount of sympathy was felt for Mrs Philpott, especially after her appearance in court, where she cut a very sorry figure. She still sported her black eye from the fracas in the *Royal Oak* and, on the whole, looked extremely frail indeed. She par-ticularly complained of suffering from severe pains in the back of her head where it had struck the step, and upon an examination by the doctor a soft spot was found. Her condition continued to worsen over the coming days, and on the morning of Thursday, 13 April she was found in an unconscious state on the floor of her bedroom. On the following Sunday she passed away without regaining consciousness.

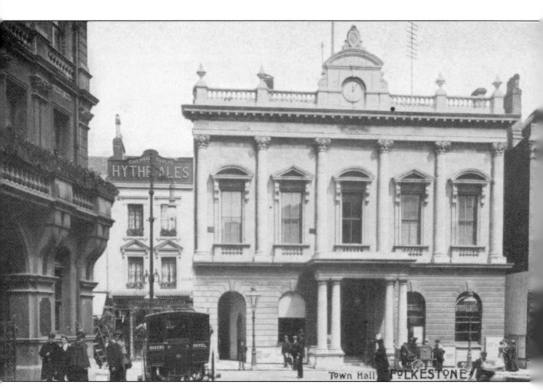

Folkestone Town Hall, where the case of Philpott v Moore was heard. Marlinova
Collection

The fracas between Moore and Mrs Philpott that led to her death took place
outside the *Royal Oak* inn in North Street, Folkestone. Folkestone Library

At the inquest into the death, the jury and coroner were seemingly at odds as to what had caused it. The jury's verdict was that 'death was accidental, caused by Moore, but in self-defence. His arm raised to protect himself, he did not strike the deceased, but she fell down accidentally.' The coroner, however, disagreed and expressed the opinion Moore had assaulted Mrs Philpott. On hearing the jury's verdict, he remarked, 'Well, gentlemen, that is your verdict, not mine'.

With public sympathy in Folkestone's fishing quarter firmly on the side of the unfortunate Mary Philpott, the berated Moore left the town to wander on his travels. A few days later Mr Philpott, who had seemingly distanced himself during the unfolding of these tragic events, found a battered old photograph of Moore hidden in a drawer amongst the clothes of his late wife.

An Off-the-Cuff Remark

Folkestone, 1904

Auguste Menn was a somewhat highly strung and unpredictable little man; he was not known as the 'Mad German' for nothing. Yet to shoot someone in cold blood was another matter. Everyone was puzzled why he had done it: had his mind finally fallen over the edge, or was an off-the-cuff remark to blame?

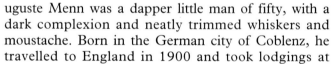uguste Menn was a dapper little man of fifty, with a dark complexion and neatly trimmed whiskers and moustache. Born in the German city of Coblenz, he travelled to England in 1900 and took lodgings at Claremont Road, Folkestone, before moving out to Court Lodge, New Barn, Lyminge. A man of independent means, his great interest in life was natural history, and he was a frequent visitor to the public library on Grace Hill, Folkestone, where he would talk at great length in broken English about the subject to whoever was prepared to listen. He was also proud to tell everyone that, because he was such a greatly educated man, he was writing a book on criminal law. However, little did poor Auguste realise that it was common knowledge around the town that he had spent some time in a German lunatic asylum suffering from hallucinations!

As the brilliant sunshine poured down during the afternoon of Thursday, 7 April 1904, both residents and visitors took the opportunity to take a stroll along Folkestone's exclusive and fashionable cliff-top promenade, The Leas, with its wonderful sea views and invigorating health-giving air. The latter would be especially beneficial to the four men from St Andrew's Convalescent Home on the East Cliff who were casually strolling along the promenade, especially 35-year-old butler William Salkeld, who was recovering from a bout of pneumonia.

As the four men approached the Leas Bandstand, two of them, Jarvis and Brooks, decided to make their way into town and left Salkeld and the other man, Harold Atkins, to continue their walk. Just past the bandstand, the two men spied the rather strange figure of Auguste Menn leaning against the cliff-top railings and as they walked past him a loud bang rang out into the air. Harold Atkins's initial thought, that his friend was playing a joke on him by dropping a firework, was quickly dispelled when Salkeld grabbed him by the arm and slumped to the ground saying he had been shot. Upon turning round, Atkins saw Menn only three or four yards away with a pistol in his hand and standing still, as if in a daze, before seemingly regaining his senses and striding off down The Leas.

Police Constables Lilley and Rew had heard the bang while patrolling the promenade, and actually saw Salkeld slump to the ground against the fence on the sea-side of the path. They quickly ran over to the scene of the crime, and on being told Menn was walking further on with a gun in his hand, Lilley ran after him. He quickly caught up with the little German, who willingly admitted it was he who had fired the gun and then handed it over to the officer without even being asked.

An ambulance was brought for the unfortunate Salkeld, who was still alive, although clearly badly injured, and he was taken to the Victoria Hospital. An examination by Doctors Wylie, Lewis and Tyson revealed the bullet had entered through the back and lodged in a kidney, causing a severe haemorrhage. It was decided

The Leas bandstand in 1904, where in that year Auguste Menn gunned down William Salkeld. Marlinova Collection

ST. ANDREW'S HOME, FOLKESTONE.

William Salkeld was recuperating at the St Andrew's Convalescent Home during his stay in Folkestone. Marlinova Collection

to try and operate to remove the bullet, but William Salkeld died the following day from peritonitis.

Auguste Menn was taken to Folkestone Police Station and his satchel was searched. In addition to some books, a snuffbox, a silver watch and chain, a railway ticket from Lyminge to Folkestone Central, a dagger and two pocket-knives were also found. After being charged with murder, the accused was placed on remand in Canterbury Prison.

Menn was obviously a highly disturbed and dangerous individual, but what had prompted him to shoot a complete stranger in the back in cold blood? Was he mad enough to pick on someone at random?

A probable motive was revealed two days later, on Saturday, 9 April at the coroner's inquest at Folkestone Town Hall, where the jury took only a minute-and-a-half to record a charge of Wilful Murder against Auguste Menn. During his evidence, Harold

Folkestone Police pictured during the Edwardian era. Marlinova Collection

Atkins revealed for the first time that he and William Salkeld had joked about Menn's appearance as they walked past him, likening him to as bookmaker because of the satchel around his shoulder. Menn had almost certainly heard the men and, with his weak and insecure mind in turmoil over what he thought was an offensive remark, decided to exact his revenge.

The case aroused great interest in an otherwise rather staid and conservative Folkestone, especially amongst the ladies who packed the public gallery in the Town Hall in the hope of catching a view of the mad little foreigner when the case was brought before the Borough Justices on Friday, 15 April. In turn, the rather vain German appeared to enjoy the attention he was receiving and responded by frequently twirling his carefully mani-cured moustache in appreciation. The finale to his 'performance' was to give his audience a great big smile when the jury ordered that Menn should be sent for trial at the County Assizes.

However, it was obvious that Menn was barking mad and he

was packed off to the asylum, where his stay was to be more permanent this time.

In stark contrast to the rather frivolous affair at the Town Hall, the victim, William Salkeld, was laid to rest in Cheriton Road Cemetery on Wednesday, 13 April amidst great solemnity. Large crowds gathered outside the Victoria Hospital to see the funeral cortege off on its way to the cemetery, although to everyone's surprise the funeral party came out from the basement rather than the front entrance. Crowds lined the route all the way to the cemetery, where several hundred people had gathered to see the beautiful coffin, with its St Andrew's Cross, lowered into the ground.

CHAPTER 19

A Year of Inexplicable Suicides

Folkestone, 1905

Three seemingly happy young men, with all to live for, bizarrely decide to end their lives in Folkestone during 1905. Two of the men were visitors to the town; one of them on honeymoon, which makes their actions seem even stranger.

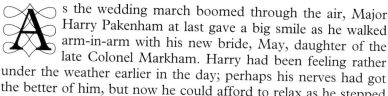 s the wedding march boomed through the air, Major Harry Pakenham at last gave a big smile as he walked arm-in-arm with his new bride, May, daughter of the late Colonel Markham. Harry had been feeling rather under the weather earlier in the day; perhaps his nerves had got the better of him, but now he could afford to relax as he stepped out of All Saints' Church, Knightsbridge into the sunny morning of Wednesday, 7 February 1905. For their honeymoon, the newlyweds had decided to stay in Folkestone (a particularly favoured resort of Harry's) and on the train down he delighted in telling his new bride what the town had to offer. Upon their arrival in Folkestone, a cab took them down to the *Royal Pavilion Hotel*, where a beautiful suite of rooms, amongst the finest the hotel had to offer, had been booked. The first evening of the couple's married life was spent listening to the orchestra in the hotel's winter garden before they retired to bed.

The next couple of days were spent sightseeing. Harry and May strolled along the leafy Lower Sandgate Road to Sandgate and went on the horse tram to Hythe, where they visited the crypt with its macabre collection of skulls and bones. One afternoon was spent listening to the band in the grounds of the Pleasure Gardens Theatre and then enjoying a sumptuous cream tea in Carlo Maestrani's restaurant in Sandgate Road. On the Friday evening before they were due to return home, Harry told May how much he had enjoyed their few days away and expressed the wish that they would return to Folkestone soon.

However, on the following morning, Saturday 11 February 1905, as they were due to book out of the hotel, Harry simply vanished. The police were informed and carried out a search of

Harry Pakenham was enjoying his honeymoon at Folkestone's sumptuous *Royal Pavilion Hotel* when he inexplicably committed suicide. Marlinova Collection

the town, but Harry was nowhere to be found. Finally, the next day, his overcoat was discovered on the beach. Inside a pocket was found a letter on *Royal Pavilion Hotel* headed paper with the words, 'Dear May, I cannot stand this awful feeling any longer and must end it. My illness I am sure is something very bad and I am nearly mad'. Five days later, the body of the unfortunate major was washed up on the same stretch of beach.

The distraught Mrs Pakenham was comforted by her husband's relatives, who then revealed to her why he may have taken his own life. During the South African War, Harry had contracted a number of fevers, which had led him to suffer a nervous breakdown. His family had hoped that his marriage to May would lead to a full recovery, but sadly this was not to be. Poor May then suffered a further tragedy when a relative, to whom she was deeply attached, passed away on the day of her husband's disappearance.

Four months on from Harry's Pakenham's sad death, Sidney Luetchford was another who was returning to Folkestone after a previous visit. The 23-year-old had greatly enjoyed his two-week holiday in Folkestone in 1903 and, fancying a break from his employment with soap manufacturers Lever Brothers in the City, booked once again with Mrs Mary Carter at 23 Penfold Road for a week's stay commencing on Saturday 17 June 1905.

Sidney duly arrived by train on the appointed day, paid his 6d tariff and proceeded to enjoy his stay in 'Fashionable Folkestone'. Mrs Carter found him to be a very quiet and amiable young man who ate his meals at regular times and came home early, and sober, every evening just in time for supper. During dinner on Thursday he excitedly told her how much he was enjoying his stay and shyly let slip that he had made the acquaintance of a very pretty young lady he had met while strolling on The Leas. They had walked down to the beach together and had enjoyed a ride on the switchback railway by the Victoria Pier before watching the pierrot show in Marine Gardens. They had arranged to meet again in the morning and Sidney could hardly contain his excitement at the prospect as he made his way out for his evening stroll.

The young man arrived back at ten o'clock for his supper and all appeared well. He was seen going upstairs to his room by Mrs

Penfold Road, Folkestone, under construction in 1896. Nine years later Sidney Luetchford took his own life at No. 23. Alan F. Taylor

2 Bournemouth Gardens, where the sad death of Charles Crosswell occurred.
Marlinova Collection

Carter some thirty minutes later just before she retired to bed. Yet in the morning, at around 7.15, she discovered the door to Sidney's room was open and his bed appeared not to have been slept in. Furthermore, downstairs, she found the front-room door was locked and, when she went outside to look through the window, found the body of her lodger slumped on the sofa. She quickly summoned her neighbour, Police Constable Smith, who got into the room through the window and discovered the young man with a pillowcase over his head and through a hole in the case a tube leading from his mouth to a gas bracket. Sidney had gassed himself, and with rigor mortis already setting in, he must have done it shortly after Mrs Carter had gone to bed. The jury at the inquest duly decided that 'the deceased had died from asphyxia, caused by coal gas poisoning, during temporary insanity.'

Yet why did this seemingly happy young man, who was due to meet his new sweetheart in the morning and had all to live for, take his own life? Had something happened on that evening stroll? Perhaps his new sweetheart had shattered all his illusions.

Just as mysterious was the death of the son of F.E. Crosswell, a well-known Folkestone builder. During the evening of Sunday, 19 November 1905 at 9.30, the dead body of sixteen-year-old Charles Creed Crosswell was found hanging in the bathroom at the family home of 2 Bournemouth Gardens. The door to the room had been locked, and when it was forced open, the deceased could be seen hanging from a hook about five feet two inches from the ground. He was fully dressed, with his arms hanging down by his side and his tongue clenched between his teeth, and he had suspended himself from the hook by using a buckled strap around his neck.

Why this apparently contented young man had committed such an act was a shock to all, although four possible theories were put forward. The obvious one was he had committed suicide, yet his family were insistent that he was always a happy, cheerful lad with a very bright disposition and not a care in the world. The dark subject of some failed sexual act was put forward; or perhaps he had tried to stretch himself to a greater height as he was the shortest one in the household. His family thought his death was connected to the fact that young Charlie fancied himself as a bit of a 'Houdini'. He kept a number of straps in his room and often asked his brothers to strap him up so he could attempt to wriggle free. Sometimes he managed it, but not always.

However, in the absence of any solid facts, the jury at the coroner's inquest returned a verdict of accidental death.

Chapter 20

A Marriage Made in Hell

Saltwood, 1908

'Nine years of misery' was how one person described the marriage of William and Margaret Bauldry, and indeed it was an unhappy time for all concerned in the relationship. Sadly, the couple's four children (another had died young) were caught in the middle of their parents' anger and dislike for each other and the condition of the children's boots was to lead to one final, tragic argument.

The marriage had taken place at Woolwich on Christmas Day 1899, and for Maggie, Bill Bauldry appeared to be a good catch. William Bauldry was born into an army family at Colchester on New Year's Day 1867 and, aged sixteen, joined the Bedfordshire Regiment at Shorncliffe Camp on 16 January 1883. However, in 1890 he was discharged from the army owing to a heart condition, although he left with a good character reference. Bauldry then took employment at Maxim's works in Erith and was still working there when he met and married Maggie.

Maggie was born Margaret Elizabeth Cloke at Saltwood, just outside Hythe, on 2 January 1876. She was the fourth of six children born to Thomas and Elizabeth Cloke (née Rolfe), who had married on 1 January 1863. At the age of eighteen Maggie had worked as a parlour maid at Hillhurst in

Margaret Bauldry, pictured when she was an employee at the Metropole Steam Laundry.
Marlinova Collection

A manacled William Bauldry
arriving at the inquest.
Marlinova Collection

Saltwood and was also in service at
the *Swan Hotel* in the High Street
at Hythe.

In 1902 Bauldry decided to
leave Maxim's and settle with his
family in Hythe. He obtained
employment at the School of
Musketry as a fatigue man, but left
in July 1903 and thereafter took on
only casual work as a labourer.
Due to her husband's reluctance to
work, Maggie took employment at
the Metropole Steam Laundry for
a time and also earned money by
bean-cutting at West Hythe and
hop-picking at Chilham. She
ended up supporting the family
virtually on her own and in
addition had to raise their children
William, May, Margaret and baby
Stephen (born 15 December
1906). Another child, John
Stanley, died on 24 September
1906 aged eighteen months, and
Maggie had also suffered a miscar-
riage that resulted in her becoming
seriously ill.

Bill and Maggie had never got
on particularly well, and by 1907
Bauldry's sullen disposition and
reluctance to work was said to
have been the reason why they had
separated on a number of occasions. The couple's extreme
poverty had led to spells in the
Elham Union workhouse and Bill
spent part of the summer of 1907
there. The *Folkestone Express* later
claimed:

*The husband was at times
extremely quarrelsome, and altogether life for the woman was
scarcely worth living, owing to his*

Maggie Bauldry tried to support her family by working at the Metropole Steam Laundry. Marlinova Collection

bad temper. He was also unemployed and not a man who appeared willing to do much to gain a good livelihood.

However, this was written when Bauldry was firmly in the dock as a wife-murderer and we can only speculate what part Maggie might have played in the breakdown of the marriage.

In October 1908 the couple were living in Horn Street, Seabrook when they decided to part once again. Bill took the three eldest children with him to his mother's house in Boxley Square, Hythe, although it was also said that William junior stayed with Maggie's brother. Not wishing to enter the workhouse, Maggie and Stephen were found lodgings by Miss Murray of the Board of Guardians, who was to support them until the separation order from Bill came through. On 6 October 1908 Maggie and Stephen moved into the downstairs front room of Albert and Nellie Wraight at 1 Franklyn Cottages, New Road, Saltwood. This was situated conveniently close to the home of Maggie's mother, Mrs Nutley, who lived in a cottage adjoining the *Castle Hotel*.

Unfortunately it was not long before Bill and Maggie were at each other's throats again. On Saturday, 10 October 1908 Maggie had seen May in Hythe wearing 'bad boots' and wrote to her husband:

Dear Bill, I hope you won't make little May run about in bad boots. Keep her indoors until I can get another pair. It makes my heart bleed to see her so. She will be a cripple – yours, Maggie.

Incensed by the note, Bauldry stormed round to New Road just before six o'clock that same day and found Maggie in the kitchen with Stephen in her arms talking to Mrs Wraight. He sat at the table thrusting the note at her and they began arguing. Bauldry went to strike her, whereupon Maggie said, 'Oh Bill, I did not think you would do that, in the weak state that I am', to which he replied, 'I was not going to hit you'.

Maggie moved to another chair, but Bauldry went and sat on the one next to her. They continued to argue and Bauldry mentioned a half-crown rent owed to Mrs Goodburn at Horn Street. He told his wife he was not going to live with her anymore and asked Mrs Wraight, 'Will you write a paper for us to sign, so that we can separate?' Mrs Wraight replied that it was not her work.

Mr Wraight then came into the kitchen and told Bauldry to stop the noise. He also asked him why he never bothered to go out to work. Wraight then went to walk down into the scullery, whereupon Bauldry hit him on the back of the head, knocking him down the steps. Bauldry then closed the door between the kitchen and the scullery, shutting Wraight out.

Maggie rushed from the kitchen with Stephen still in her arms, but Bauldry caught hold of her at the bottom of the stairs. Mrs Wraight saw him fumbling about in his trouser-pocket and called her husband for help before running out into the back garden to shout to her neighbour John Morris. Mr Wraight (who was still in the scullery) returned to the kitchen, and looking towards the bottom of the stairs saw Maggie and Stephen being pinned down by Bauldry, who was brandishing a knife. Wraight attempted to pull Bauldry off them, but being unable to do so went outside looking for help.

Meanwhile, Morris, who worked as an engine driver and general labourer for Hythe Corporation, had heard the quarrelling and told his daughter to fetch a policeman. Mr Wraight had decided to do the same and ran to fetch PC George Willson, who lived about two minutes away. As Wraight walked away from the house he saw Bauldry head off in the direction of Sandling Junction station.

William Bauldry had stabbed his wife twice with the knife. Maggie, still holding baby Stephen in her arms, managed to make her way into the kitchen before she collapsed.

Mrs Wraight went to fetch the district nurse, Lizzie Hooper (who was out), and upon her return found Morris in the kitchen. He had discovered Maggie lying on the kitchen floor, her head overhanging the step down into the scullery, with a severe wound to her throat and a cut chin. She was still conscious and asked for

The fatal disagreement between the Bauldrys took place at this house in Saltwood. Brenda Howlett

Albert and Nellie Wraight pictured outside their house, where the murder took place. Marlinova Collection

something on her stomach as she was in great pain. The baby, who was still in her arms, was fortunately uninjured and was passed by Morris to Mrs Wraight before he went off to fetch some brandy for poor Maggie. A trail of blood could be seen where she had dragged herself along the floor.

PC Willson and Lizzie Hooper arrived at the house and found Maggie barely alive. She managed to say to the nurse, 'I am dying, he's done for me,' and Miss Hooper, seeing the severity of the wounds, asked for Dr Clifford Hackney to be fetched from Hythe. However, Maggie passed away before the doctor could arrive.

Bauldry, meanwhile, had made his way down Dark Lane to his mother's house. At 7.20 p.m. he entered the tap room of the *Gate Inn* and asked for a whisky. He was joined by his mother, who asked him, 'Is it true, Bill?' to which he replied, 'Yes; I have got to be handed over'. Bauldry was about to return to the bar when PC Willson came into the pub and placed him under arrest. He was then walked through the High Street to Seabrook Police Station and on the following day was charged with the murder of his wife, to which he casually replied, 'She's dead, then'.

The inquest into the death of Margaret Bauldry took place at Saltwood Village Hall two days after the murder on Monday, 12 October 1908. Bill Bauldry claimed that his wife had fallen on the knife, although he also said at one point, 'I must admit I done it, but ...' before the coroner stopped him from finishing the sentence and urged him only to question the witnesses. The prisoner appeared to relish the atten-tion he was getting and laughed and joked with the policeman by his side. The only time his composure was jolted was when his mother ran up and said, 'Mercy on you' as she embraced him.

PC George Willson, who arrested William Bauldry. *Marlinova Collection*

The *Gate Inn*, Hythe, where William Bauldry was arrested for the murder of his wife. David Harper

Bauldry also took studious interest in the statements of the witnesses, who included Nellie and Albert Wraight, John Morris, Lizzie Hooper, George Willson and Clifford Hackney. He denied hitting Mr Wraight and accused him and his wife of failing to stop him and running away. However, he was told by the coroner not to ask those sorts of questions and stick to the facts.

The jury took less than a minute to decide William Bauldry was guilty of murdering his wife, and in the adjourned meeting the following Wednesday the prisoner was committed for trial at Maidstone Assizes. On the same day Maggie Bauldry was laid to rest in the quiet churchyard of St Peter and St Paul, Saltwood. A large crowd lined the route from the house in New Road, where her body had remained since the murder, to the church and every household drew down their blinds.

William Bauldrey's trial came up before the assizes in November 1908 in front of Judge Hon. Sir E. Ridley. H.H. Lawless and W.R. Briggs appeared for the prosecution and H.C. Harbord for the defence. The Clerk of the Court read out a long statement by Bauldry, who had grown a beard and moustache, in which he claimed the stabbing was an accident. He claimed Maggie had been a very good wife and mother to their children and that he had no reason to harm her. He was heartbroken that his children no longer had a mother and asked for merciful treatment as he had suffered from a 'diseased head' for two years and had a heart condition.

Nevertheless, Bauldry was found guilty after thirty minutes' deliberation by the jury, although they recommended grounds for mercy because the stabbing had been carried out in a moment of frenzy. However, Judge Ridley put on the traditional black cap and sentenced William Bauldry to be hanged. On being asked if he had anything to say he replied, 'No, sir, only that I am innocent, that is all'.

The date of the execution was fixed for Tuesday, 8 December 1908. William was visited by his ever-loyal mother on the Saturday before the execution and he composed this rather touching last letter to a friend at Erith:

> *Dear Joe, I write these few lines to you, wishing you and your wife and family quite well. You have acted a good friend, and I hope and trust to God you and your wife and family will live to enjoy this world for years to come. I shall be gone from this world when you get this letter, and I can truthfully go knowing you have done your best. My mother came on Saturday last. It has quite broken her heart, poor old soul. She has been a good mother to me. I told her to send you one of my photos. I have bared [sic] up since this sad affair. I feel sorry leaving my mother and little children; but I know the children will be well looked after. Give my love to all old friends, Joe, and tell them my last words. I wish them all well – from your old friend, Bill Bauldry. Good-bye, good-bye.*

Having slept little the night before, Bauldry was visited by the prison chaplain, Reverend E. Stevens, at six o'clock and after a light breakfast partook of Holy Communion. A few minutes before eight o'clock he was fetched by the executioner Pierrepoint and walked to his place of execution with dignity and with his head held high. William Bauldry was executed in the clothes he had worn during his trial and was laid to rest within the prison grounds.

CHAPTER 21

Behind Respectable Curtains

Sandgate, 1908

This is a tragic case of a respectable Sandgate woman taking the life of her daughter and then attempting to take her own. Having married into one of Sandgate's leading and most respected families, Mrs Anne Kenward's crime rocked the tightly knit seaside village to its core. Life in the Kenward household on the days leading up to the tragedy appeared to be quite straightforward and held no clues as to why the killing took place. However, it was soon to emerge that problems within the family had been furtively hidden behind the curtains of that comfortable and upright Edwardian home.

Mr and Mrs Frederick William Kenward and their daughter Freda lived at 6 Knoll Gardens, The Crescent, Sandgate. Mr Kenward was employed as a grocer's assistant at his brother's shop at 95 Sandgate High Street, just five minutes' walk from the house. He was captain of the village cricket team and a respected local figure. In addition to owning the grocery shop, Fred's brother, Mr H.D. Kenward, was a Sandgate councillor. Mrs Anne Elizabeth Kenward, née Hall, was thirty-four years old and came from nearby Seabrook. She had been married to her husband for four years and their daughter, Freda Elizabeth, was born on 25 October 1907.

On the morning of 29 December 1908, Mr Kenward left the house at the usual time of 8 a.m. to walk the short distance to the shop. He returned home around two hours later before starting his grocery round and stayed for five minutes to down a quick cup of tea. At 2 p.m. he came back to the house for his dinner, which he shared with his wife. She appeared to be in good spirits and even offered to dry his wet boots. When he left at 2.45 p.m. to begin another round, his wife flung her arms around him and expressed the wish that he did not have to go back out into the wet and miserable weather. After kissing young Freda, Mr Kenward rode out into the gloomy day, stopping as he turned the corner to acknowledge his wife and daughter waving him off.

Fred and Anne Kenward, pillars of respectability in the Sandgate Cricket Club. Alan F. Taylor

At six o'clock Fred Kenward was glad to be getting home after a wet and tiring day delivering groceries around Sandgate and its immediate area. At almost a trotting pace he crossed Sandgate High Street into The Crescent, but upon turning the corner he was surprised to find the house in darkness. As he approached the front door, all was eerily still. This was most unusual, for Freda would normally be having her bath at this time and, as she especially loved her bathtime, would be generating a lot of noise.

Upon entering the house he called out to his wife, but received no answer. After a quick look downstairs he climbed the stairs up to the main bedroom, where he half-expected to find his wife and daughter having a nap on the bed. What greeted him instead was a scene of the utmost horror. Anne and Freda were indeed lying on the bed, but with their throats cut and their clothes and bed covers saturated with blood. Poor little Freda was dead, but Mrs Kenward was still alive and upon seeing her husband asked him for a glass of

A newspaper advertisement for the Kenward shop at Christmas 1908.
Folkestone Herald

The Kenwards' grocer's shop can just be seen to the left of the lamppost. Alan F. Taylor

water. After giving his wife the drink, Mr Kenward noticed a bloodstained razor on the bedside table: this had obviously been the instrument used to commit this horrendous act.

Unable to believe his eyes and the situation he found himself in, Mr Kenward rushed over to the house opposite and recounted his traumatic experience to Adam Keeler and his daughter, saying, 'I am in great trouble, do come, do come. My wife and child are lying on the bed smothered in blood.' The Keelers rushed over to the Kenward house, but upon the seeing the carnage in the bedroom, Miss Keeler decided to fetch a doctor as a matter of urgency. Unfortunately the local doctor, Dr Bradley, was out on a call, but a man at the surgery volunteered to find another.

Meanwhile, back at the house, an understandably distraught Fred Kenward did his best to comfort his wife. His initial thought that they had been violently attacked was dispelled, however, after he found a note on the writing table in the front room. Written by his wife, as an apparent suicide note, it said, 'Dear mother and sisters, please forgive me for trouble causing. I can stand it no longer.'

Mrs Kenward's mother and sister arrived at the house from their home at 3 Darnley Terrace, just five minutes away. Dr Harold Fairrie of RAMC Shorncliffe Camp, who had been called out by Dr Bradley's surgery, followed them in. He examined little Freda first, and confirmed she was dead, before examining Mrs Kenward. He found the razor had been used in both cases to inflict a three- to four-inch wound extending transversely across the throat.

Eventually, Dr Fairrie left and Dr Bradley arrived, and requested a nurse be brought in to stay with Mrs Kenward. The pitiable woman was later taken to hospital and the body of the child was removed. With his mind in turmoil over the horror of the day's events, Mr Kenward was left to clean up the bedroom with the help of his wife's family.

The inquest on the death of Freda Elizabeth Kenward took place on 1 January 1909 at the Sandgate Public Offices with coroner R.H. Mercer presiding. Mr T.H. Goddard was chosen as the foreman of the jury and Mr Martin Mowill represented the Kenward family. The tiny room allowed for only a few spectators in addition to the jury, witnesses and the police. These included the Reverend E.V.E. Bryan (the Vicar of Sandgate), Dr Bradley, Superintendent Hollands of Folkestone Police, and Mr H.D. Kenward. The latter had received so many condolences on the loss of his daughter he was forced to take out an advertisement in the *Folkestone Herald* pointing out that he was not in fact the baby's father!

The coroner questioned Fred Kenward about his movements on the day of the murder, much to the interest of Hollands, who regarded him as a possible suspect in the case. Mr Kenward described the day in detail, before being asked about his wife's state of mind. He revealed that although she presented a contented face to the world, the child's teething and general fret-fulness at times caused her mother sleepless nights. This in turn made her irritable and depressed.

Mr Kenward then went on to reveal another problem the family

The Kenward house in The Crescent, Sandgate. Baby Freda was killed in the front bedroom on the first floor. Marlinova Collection

had faced. Despite giving his wife all of his earnings, she had still run up debts at several shops and had got the family into financial difficulties, much to his embarrassment.

However, Mr Kenward's revelations about his wife's difficulties with money did not go down at all well with her relatives. His sister-in-law Daisy Hall claimed Fred Kenward deceived his wife over money when they got married and she was often left to go short. Furthermore, she alleged he had deceived her family when asking for Anne Kenward's hand in marriage by saying he was an equal partner in the Kenward grocery business when in fact he was not! Therefore he had exaggerated his earning potential, and as a result Mrs Kenward's parents were forced to assist financially with her debts. Her sister had confided to her that the marriage was not a happy one (and it's interesting to note that Anne Kenward's suicide note was addressed to her family, not to her husband).

In his summing up, the coroner asked the jury not to judge Anne Kenward's sanity, but to establish whether the child was killed by her mother. Following a brief deliberation, the jury decided Freda Elizabeth had met her death at the hands of her mother. The prisoner was then committed on the coroner's warrant.

On 2 February 1909 Mrs Kenward was summoned to appear at Seabrook Police Court. She was accompanied by a nurse and wore a thick black veil that totally obscured her features from view. On the bench sat Mr J. Du Boulay and Mr F.E. Burke, and Mr Mowill was retained to defend Mrs Kenward. Apart from a clerk who was taking notes for the defence, the only other people in the court were Fred Kenward, a few close relatives and the police. The Clerk of the Court read the charge that on 29 December 1908 in the parish of Sandgate, Mrs Anne Elizabeth Kenward did feloniously, and with malice aforethought, kill and murder one Freda Elizabeth Kenward.

The first witness to speak was Police Sergeant Cockrell, who was stationed at Seabrook Police Station. He recalled that he was sent to investigate the crime and told the prisoner that she would be taken into custody and charged with the wilful murder of her daughter, to which she made no reply. He further added that she was to be charged with attempting to commit suicide in the parish. When asked if she understood the charges, Mrs Kenward replied, 'Yes'.

Due to the serious nature of the crime, Superintendent Hollands applied to have Mrs Kenward remanded in custody until noon the following Tuesday when she would appear at Canterbury Crown Court. However, while Mr Du Boulay and Mr Burke were supplying the remand papers, Mrs Kenward collapsed on the floor in front of the dock. Fortunately, following treatment by her nurse, she was able to get back to her feet and was returned in custody to Canterbury Prison.

Nevertheless, back at the prison, the health of Anne Kenward continued to deteriorate and later that evening she died. The

Seabrook Police Court, where Mrs Kenward was detained following the murder of her daughter. Peter and Annie Bamford

inquest on her death at the Municipal Offices in Canterbury before the City Coroner, Dr T.S. Johnson, found she had died as a result of injuries inflicted while attempting to take her own life.

The brothers Kenward, and their business, never got over the shock of the crime and moved away. Both the shop and the house can still be seen; the latter slumbering in a quiet crescent off the main A259 coast road, giving no outward clue to the tragedy that once took place behind those respectable curtains.

CHAPTER 22

The Nursery Rhyme Crime

Shorncliffe, 1920

This is a sad case of infanticide where the mother was allowed to get away with the crime, even though her guilt appeared to be clearly established. However, in a strange twist to the tale, the staid respectability of the old Cinque Port of Hythe was shaken when the identification of the murdered baby's father was revealed.

On Friday, 14 May 1920, three soldiers returning to Somerset Barracks at Shorncliffe Camp were crossing War Department land near Sandy Lane when they noticed some bracken had been tied down. Upon close inspection a white cloth could be seen covering the ground, and when a corner was lifted, a child's hand was revealed.

The police were called to the scene and, upon lifting the cloth, discovered the body of a baby lying under a blackthorn bush and covered with dead bracken and fern leaves. When these were removed it was found that the baby was clothed in a white cotton gown, which was also covering its face, and two nappies pinned together with a safety pin. When the gown was pulled away from the face, it shockingly revealed a piece of white silk had been rammed into the mouth as a gag and a handkerchief was tied over the nose and mouth. Lying beside the body was a piece of paper containing a nursery rhyme, and during a search of the area further sheets of rhymes were discovered.

An examination of the body by Dr W.B. Chubb revealed it to be that of a male infant two or three months old with brown hair. The cause of death had been by suffocation three to eight days before the body was discovered. Three marks on the left arm indicated that the child had been vaccinated eight or ten days before death.

Enquires by the police soon led them to apprehend Amy Esther Minnie Price; a 21-year-old housekeeper living at her place of work at 30 Mill Road, Hythe. When asked the whereabouts of her baby she initially replied he was staying with friends in Ashford. However, on being told she was being taken to Seabrook Police

Station to verify this information, she offered to tell the truth: namely that the baby had died in her arms gasping for breath. Nevertheless, further questioning led to Miss Price being charged on Tuesday, 18 May with the murder of her baby son William Frank Price by suffocation between 1 and 14 May 1920, and she was remanded in custody.

The case was brought before the coroner at Seabrook on Saturday, 5 June, and Henrietta Halsall, the Head Nurse at the South Canterbury Infirmary, revealed Miss Price had been admitted to the infirmary on 1 March in a state of pregnancy. The baby had subsequently been born on 6 April and was registered as an illegitimate child. Mother and baby were discharged on 1 May and had caught the 9.48 a.m. Elham Valley line train to Shorncliffe, where they were seen upon the train's arrival at 10.25 a.m. by the ticket collector Herbert Savage.

Miss Emily Moore, who resided next-door to Miss Price at 28 Mill Road, then told her story of the events of 1 May. Upon hearing that Miss Price had returned from Canterbury, she had gone round to see her and the baby, yet was stunned to be told the

Shorncliffe railway station, where young William Price was last sighted.
Marlinova Collection

The body of William Price was found just off lonely Sandy Lane, close to Shorncliffe Camp. Marlinova Collection

The house of shame in Hythe, where Amy Price became pregnant by her employer. Marlinova Collection

baby had died at four days old. She was further startled by her friend's revelation that the baby had resembled Mr Maycock, who was head of the house and Amy Price's employer!

The police alleged what happened was simply that Miss Price had walked from Shorncliffe station with the baby to the murder spot nearly two miles distant and then murdered him by stuffing the gag into his mouth.

After hearing all the evidence, the coroner's jury was asked to give their verdict. Their initial, and fuddled, decision that the child was wilfully murdered but they could not decide by whom, proved unsatisfactory to the coroner, who asked them to exercise their common sense and sent them away to reconsider their decision. They returned the second time with the verdict of 'wilful murder of William Frank Price by his mother' and the prisoner was sent for trial at the Kent County Assizes in Maidstone on Tuesday, 22 June 1920.

At the trial, where the prisoner pleaded not guilty, Mr Maycock stunned all present by revealing that he was indeed the father of the murdered baby, but could not understand why Miss Price would want to keep the baby from him. The prosecution argued it was an open-and-shut case against the accused, yet the defence counsel countered strongly that it had not even been proved conclusively that the murdered baby was indeed the prisoner's child. The summing-up by the presiding judge appeared to favour the accused. He stated that her half-truths should not be held against her, and this appeared to sway the minds of the jury, who returned after twenty minutes with a Not Guilty verdict.

CHAPTER 23

The House of Horror

Cheriton, 1934

It was once described as England's most haunted place, and the ghostly happenings at Underhill House, Cheriton have featured in many Kent ghost books. However, the actual tragedies that took place at the house – there has been at least one murder and four suicides, which may well account for all the strange goings-on – have been less well documented.

Originally erected in 1840 and once owned by the Brockman family of Beachborough, the house was later used to accommodate the brigadier in charge of Shorncliffe Camp. Yet, in spite of the house being destroyed by fire in 1978, its site is still reputedly haunted to this day.

Robert Alured Denne appeared to have all he wanted in life. Born on 15 September 1838 into a wealthy family, his chosen profession was the Royal Navy and he had risen to the rank of lieutenant before leaving the service at the age of twenty-five in 1863. That same year he married his sweetheart, Emma Honeywood, and having obtained the post of Cornet in the East Kent Yeomanry decided to settle down at Underhill House, a handsome villa residence somewhat isolated, tucked away in the valley behind St Martin's Plain, Cheriton.

Set in 1.46 acres with spacious accommodation for three reception rooms, four principal bedrooms and two bathrooms, as well as housing domestic quarters comprising four bedrooms, a bathroom and a kitchen/servants' hall, this fine house appeared to commensurate with the rising status of the wealthy young man. He had acquired a particular interest in property and land, becoming a leading member of the Fair Trade Movement in Kent and overseeing a profitable grazing business on his land on the Romney Marsh. Living life to the full, Alured was also an enthusiastic member of the East Kent Hunt (which was based at Underhill), a Justice of the Peace and an active member of the Conservative Party.

Yet, lurking behind its unassuming facade, the curse of the

Underhill House, 'The House of Horror', can be seen in the background of this photograph. Peter and Annie Bamford

house unfortunately began to make its mark. Within a short time of moving into the house, Alured was delighted to discover that his wife was pregnant, but sadly the baby died in infancy and he seemed never to be the same man again. He began to suffer from regular bouts of severe depression, brought on, it is said, not only by the loss of the baby but also by the premonitions he was having foretelling absolute financial ruin to all those involved in agriculture.

Emma tried desperately to calm his fears, yet her husband continued on a downward spiral. He began to suffer from epileptic fits, and although these were brought largely under control by powerful administrations of nitrate of silver, that particular remedy gave his complexion a peculiar bluish hue that heightened his insecurity even more. To add to his woes, he suffered from pains in his leg brought about when a horse lashed out and broke it while he was hunting out at Acrise in 1881.

Alured blamed all his troubles on the house, which he thought was cursed by an evil presence, and entertained thoughts of moving out. However, this was never to happen, for in 1887 Alured took his own life.

The military at Shorncliffe Camp eventually took over the house and it became the home of the Camp Brigadier. However, it still continued to inflict torment on its occupants, as evidenced by two rather shadowy suicides that were said to have subsequently taken place there. The first involved an army officer, who, heavily in debt through gambling, shot himself in the entrance hall outside the commander's office. Later, an army padre hanged himself in an airing cupboard off the main corridor because he thought he would no longer be required following the amalgamation of regiments at the camp. Pitiably, the padre, having become aware of the house's unfortunate past, had tried to cure it of its malediction with exorcism, only to become a victim of it himself. Another person was said to have hung himself in the stable block.

However, the most notorious event in the story of this most unfortunate of buildings occurred on Monday, 1 May 1934. A 37-year-old maid named May Hiett was found strangled in a

Following his murder of May Hiett, Charles Jay went to the *Britannia Inn* in Horn Street. Marlinova Collection

bedroom, while in another bedroom the Brigadier's valet, forty-year-old Charles Jay, was found suffering from a gunshot wound from which he never recovered.

During the previous evening Jay had asked Brigadier W.N. Herbert if he could escort Miss Hiett out of the camp as it was her birthday. Permission was granted; however, another member of staff, named Louisa Grenville, saw Jay and Miss Hiett discussing their evening out and thought the maid seemed reluctant to go. Miss Grenville then left the house after arranging with Jay for him to leave the door key on the windowsill, but upon her return at 9 p.m. she found the key was not there and the house was locked and in darkness. Jay eventually appeared to let her in, but fearing something was amiss, Miss Grenville offered to take a hot water bottle up to May. However, Jay unconvincingly replied she had gone out to a shop and the bottle would be cold by the time she got back.

The site of Underhill House today; looking across to the surviving barn.
Courtesy of Major Carpenter, 2nd Infantry Brigade

An agitated Jay was later seen at the *Britannia Inn*, Horn Street, quickly downing a pint of beer, and again at 11.15 p.m. by the Brigadier, who remarked how unusual it was to see him up so late and writing a letter.

Early the next morning, Miss Grenville saw Jay coming into the kitchen from the garden brandishing a gun, before he disappeared upstairs. On reaching his bedroom the valet, when called by the Brigadier, replied, 'I am busy for the minute, ask May to bring your tea,' before it was believed he shot himself, although no one heard a sound. The Brigadier's call to May remained unanswered and when he went upstairs to find out why, he found her bedroom door locked. After finding a key to open it, he found the maid was covered with a nightgown, and upon pulling it back saw that she was dead. A visit to Jay's bedroom found him suffering from the gunshot wound from which he never recovered.

In all probability, Jay strangled May Hiett around 8 p.m. on the Sunday in a fit of jealousy over their floundering relationship. The hot-tempered valet had been roused by rumours May had been seen kissing another man, and by the coolness she had recently shown him. The Brigadier later found on his desk the letter Jay had been writing the previous evening, which said: 'Dear Sir, I am sorry to cause you all this trouble, also poor dearest May. As you know I like May very much. There are many people after her.'

The jury at the inquest returned the verdict that May Hiett was murdered by Charles Jay, who then committed suicide.

Yet, in spite of its haunted reputation, a visit to the site of the house on a warm summer's evening found it anything but intimidating. Still beautifully situated along a narrow lane surrounded by fields and a bank of trees, the layout of the house can still be discerned by surviving brickwork. From the house there is a wonderful view looking across the valley to Horn Street. The stable, where a gruesome hanging was said to have taken place, still remains in use and on our visit a friendly white horse came out to greet us. It all seemed a million miles away from the woes of Alured Denne, Charles Jay and possessed padres.

CHAPTER 24

The Dover Trunk Murder

Dover, 1936

Gladys Varley's life was a complete disaster. True, she had brought it all on herself, but it is still hard not to feel some compassion for her. Have given birth to six children in less than eight years Gladys was left to cope with the hardships of life as the men around her disappeared off into the sunset. As she knocked the workhouse door again, she decided there was only one thing left to do.

Gladys Varley was, sadly, one of those people who are destined for an unfortunate time on this earth. Perhaps it was something to do with her family's ill-fated background that was responsible. The daughter of Mr and Mrs Revell of 129 St Radigund's Road, Dover, Gladys's grandfather had hung himself in 1904, as did her uncle in 1920. At the

129 St Radigund's Street, Dover; once the home of baby-murderer Gladys Varley. Marlinova Collection

age of seventeen she became pregnant and, to save face, married the father on 2 October 1927. A little girl was born on 26 December 1927, and Gladys is known subsequently to have given up another girl for adoption. A son was born on 14 March 1932, but in the following month her husband walked out, leaving Gladys with nothing. She was forced to seek relief and along with her children spent frequent spells in the workhouse.

In 1933 Gladys met a serving member of the Royal Air Force and they had a daughter, Joyce, born in May 1934. She became pregnant again just after the following Christmas, whereupon her lover left for Sudan with the RAF. Needless to say, nothing was heard from him again. Gladys was forced to enter the workhouse, and on 28 September 1935 she gave birth to twin boys there. Although registered as Peter and David, Gladys was soon calling the boys William and Brian.

On 8 October 1935 she was discharged from the workhouse with five children under eight in tow, although Gladys was in no position to offer them any kind of decent upbringing. As well as having little money, she was lazy and a somewhat compulsive liar and furthermore, apart from little Joycey, appeared to hold no real affection for her children. Almost from birth the twins were looked after by her friend Mrs Winifred Barringer, and in January 1936 the authorities had no choice but to place the two eldest children in a Dr Barnardo's home. Gladys and Joyce then joined the twins and Mrs Barringer at the home of Mrs Martha Wilson at 2 Elizabeth Street, Dover.

However, in the following month, Gladys found that her outdoor relief had been suspended, and on 27 February got a ticket for the workhouse. She was urged to enter the institution for the sake of her children by Inspector Harold Fletcher of the NSPCC. but refused to do so. Instead, she found new lodgings the next day with Mrs Frances Niccolls at 149 Snargate Street, costing 7s per week with light. Calling herself Mrs Revell, she spun Mrs Niccolls a few yarns, telling her she had only one child and her husband was in the Royal Scots but had no sleeping-out pass. By telling Mrs Niccolls she had only one child (perhaps this was a condition of the lodging?) had Gladys already decided to carry out what was to follow?

Gladys used the babies' pram and a trunk to move her belongings from Elizabeth Street and on the following day (Saturday, 29 February) collected the twins from Mrs Barringer. She returned to Mrs Wilson and Mrs Barringer the next day, so that they could look after Joyce, but did not bring the twins with her. Upon being asked where they were, she told them her landlady's daughter

The Dover Workhouse, where Gladys Varley was a frequent visitor. Bob Hollingsbee

Kitty had taken them down to the seafront. When Mrs Wilson took Joyce back to Snargate Street at 6.30 p.m. Gladys told her she couldn't come in because a soldier named Jim McPhee was having a lie-down. The only soldier who lodged in the house, however, was called David Reid Watson.

Mrs Wilson returned to see Gladys in the morning, but upon asking after the twins was told they were upstairs in a pram and should not be disturbed. This was puzzling, as Gladys's room was downstairs and those upstairs were let to other tenants.

For the remainder of the week, Mrs Wilson, now seriously worried about their whereabouts and health, attempted to see the twins, but to no avail. She warned Gladys, 'If you have done anything to them or there is anything the matter with them; you will get your knuckles rapped, and rapped sore.' Gladys retorted: 'What the ___ do you take me for? I may be a rogue, but not a murderer.'

Harold Fletcher was alerted and on Wednesday, 4 March called round to the house in company with his superintendent. They too were told that the twins were upstairs. On one occasion Gladys made her excuses to check on them, but upon being asked if they could see them she made the excuse that they were fast asleep.

On the following Friday Mrs Wilson came round to the house again, but upon finding Gladys was out, took the opportunity to have a look round with Mrs Niccolls. The landlady was astonished when told there should be twins in the house, as she had never seen or heard them, and of course she had been told by Gladys that her only child was Joyce. They saw the pram in the wash-house, but there was no sign of the twins. Two days later Gladys and Joyce visited Mrs Wilson and stayed for dinner. When Mr Wilson asked of the twins, Gladys replied with the curious state-ment, 'Walls have ears', and told them that a Miss Hobman had taken the twins away.

The disappearance of the twins was fast becoming the talk of Dover. On Tuesday, 10 March Gladys bumped into David Reid Watson opposite the *Clarendon* inn in Snargate Street and they went for a walk. He told her he had heard in the barracks that she had twins, but Gladys denied it saying, 'I have only one, and that's Joycey'.

Nevertheless, even Gladys knew that this pretence could not go on for ever. On the morning of Friday, 13 March at 11.45 she was summoned to the police station to be interviewed about another matter. When asked about her children, she told the officer she wanted to 'make a clean breast of it'. She volunteered to make the following statement, written down at her dictation:

> *I had got no money to feed them with. The relief people refused to give me any. Joyce was alright. Mrs Wilson gave her some food, but the other two, well, they died. They are still at Mrs Niccolls'. They died a week ago on Monday last* [8 March]. *They are in my room at Mrs Niccolls's house, lying on the bed.*

The police went to search the bedroom, but found nothing. However, during a thorough search of the house they discovered a trunk hidden behind the wash-house door. The label on it had been partially torn yet 'Mrs Varley 129 St Radi' could still be made out. This was the same trunk Gladys had used to move her belongings from Mrs Wilson's house. Upon breaking open the trunk the police discovered the bodies of the twins lying under a pillow. They were dressed in the same clothes they had worn on 29 February when they were collected from Mrs Barringer.

The bodies were formally identified by Mr Barringer, and were

examined by Dr Joseph Richardson, the police surgeon. He
concluded they had been dead for at least a week, but no longer
than a fortnight. However, it seems almost certain that the twins
were killed on 29 February as soon as they arrived at 149 Snargate
Street (to hide their existence from Mrs Niccolls) rather than 8
March, as Gladys claimed. Both boys were found to be severely
undernourished, although Peter (William) at eight pounds eight
ounces was considerably larger than David (Brian) at six pounds
three ounces (they should have weighed between twelve and
fifteen pounds). Death was due to asphyxia caused by strangulation. This was done by means of a cord tied tightly around the
neck, although Peter also had a white silk ribbon tied forcefully
around his neck that had come from his vest. As he was the bigger
of the twins this was perhaps done to ensure that he was dead.

Gladys was charged with the murder of her two children
between 29 February and 13 March 1936 and was bound over to
appear at Dover Magistrates' Court the next day. She was found

Snargate Street, the scene of the Dover Trunk Murder in 1936. *Marlinova
Collection*

guilty and committed for trial at the Central Criminal Court, Old Bailey on 21 April.

The trial was actually held on Thursday, 23 April and took place before Mr Justice Finlay. Gladys pleaded not guilty, and the prosecution counsel Mr Eustace Fulton announced that only the charge in respect of David Varley would be proceeded with. Although her defence tried in vain to garner some sympathy from the jury by highlighting her wretched life, Gladys was found guilty and sentenced to hang. However, by now, Gladys's plight had amassed considerable compassion amongst the general public and her sentence was commuted to life imprisonment.

So at last a bit of good fortune had come Gladys's way for, within the next few months, two other women, Dorothea Waddingham and Charlotte Bryant, were both to be hung for their crimes.

CHAPTER 25

The Whiting That Got Away

Dover 1936 and Folkestone 1938

Far removed from the select world of Folkestone's West End during the 1930s was its seamier underworld of petty crime and prostitution, frequented by men such as Bill Whiting. This particular ne'er-do-well was renowned for his quick temper and violent tendencies; that's why he was known as 'Wiscous' [sic]. His rather aimless life reached a bizarre climax during the late 1930s when his estranged wife was murdered by his rival for her love, and then two years later Whiting himself was put on trial for murdering a part-time prostitute, but somehow contrived to get away with it.

Poor Ellen Whiting led a dull life of drudgery and hardship. Left to struggle to bring up three children while her husband drifted between unemployment and menial casual work, what little money he earned usually never found its way into her pocket. As Bill put on his dark jacket and green scarf and sauntered off to yet another appointment with the pub, Ellen looked at herself and the poor state she was in and realised she was sinking faster than one of Bill's pints.

So she decided to do something about it, and during the

Mrs Ellen Whiting, murdered by George Bryant in Dover in 1936.
Dover Express

The arrow marks the room at 301 London Road, Dover, where George Bryant murdered Ellen Whiting on 16 May 1936. Marlinova Collection

high summer of 1935 began an affair with an acquaintance of her husband named George Bryant: a 39-year-old Cheriton man who was also married. Bill Whiting soon found out about his wife's affair, but she carried on with it regardless and in December 1935 was persuaded by Bryant that they should set up home together. Taking her two youngest children with them, 'Mr and Mrs Bryant' set up home together in a flat at 301 London Road, Dover.

Sadly for Ellen, her dreams of new-found happiness were quickly dispelled when her new partner turned out to be just as bad as, if not worse than, her husband. Bryant, who refused to work, spent any money they had on drink and his resulting behaviour led them into constant trouble with their landlord. She had simply exchanged one bad apple for another, but unfortunately there appeared to be no escape: Bryant had warned her she would only be allowed to leave him over his dead body.

Nevertheless, she intermittently met up with her husband and on 16 May 1936 they went for a drink in Folkestone, where Whiting asked her to go back to him. Ellen promised an answer within in a week's time, when they arranged to meet again, but Bryant found out about the intended meeting, and, seething with rage, promised himself he was going to ensure it would never take place.

Five days later, on Thursday, 21 May, at around 5.40 p.m., PC Simpson was on duty at Folkestone Police Station when Bryant walked in and said, 'I wish to give myself up for causing the death of Mrs E. Whiting at 301 London Road, Dover this afternoon at about 4.30 p.m.' After being cautioned, he continued, 'I am guilty. I hit her over the head with a bottle and afterwards strangled her. I sent the children to the pictures, as they would be out of the way.'

A search of Bryant's trousers and jacket revealed extensive bloodstains splattered all over them and a wet patch where he had tried in vain to wash some of the stains off. When asked why he had done it, Bryant replied, 'I was looking for someone else to do in. Ellen was one of the straightest women on this earth and she is married to that bastard Wiscous Whiting. When you see him tell him he had a narrow escape.' Later that evening, Bryant was handed over to the Dover Police.

Within ten minutes of Bryant entering Folkestone Police Station and confessing all, a call was made to their Dover counterparts to search the attic room where the couple lived. Finding the door locked, they broke it open and found the dead body of Mrs Whiting covered in blood and surrounded by pieces of glass from a broken beer bottle. Extensive wounds could be seen on both her head and wrists and a stocking was tightly tied around her neck. Dr Joseph Richardson was called upon to examine the body and he deduced she had indeed been killed around 4.30 p.m. (as stated by Bryant), by strangulation with the stocking, after being knocked unconscious with the beer bottle. The blood found on Bryant's clothes was matched to that from Ellen Whiting.

At Dover Police Station, Bryant willingly gave an account of what had happened. He claimed he had spent the early part of the afternoon drinking in a local pub and had taken a pint bottle of beer home with him to share with Ellen. He was seen by his landlady, Mrs Marie Griggs, returning to his flat at 2.30 p.m. and after being asked if he had come home for trouble, replied with the curious remark, 'I deserve everything'. Unable to carry out his original objective of murdering Bill Whiting, he had now set his sights on killing Ellen and soon after arriving back home sent the children to pictures on the pretext he wanted a quiet drink with their mother. His immediate plan to murder her was thwarted when an insurance agent named Kenneth Buckwell called at between 3 and 3.30 p.m. (and in doing so became the last person to see Ellen Whiting alive), but about an hour later Bryant grabbed the beer bottle and carried out his horrible assignment. He then left and locked the room, leaving the key on the landing washstand, where the police later discovered it, before making his way to Folkestone.

Bryant was charged with the murder of Ellen Whiting later that evening and appeared at Dover Police Court on Wednesday, 3 June in a hearing that lasted three hours. The accused continued to plead guilty and refused all legal aid, preferring to conduct his own defence. During a particularly heated exchange when he questioned Bill Whiting, he retorted, 'Now I will show you how to take punishment, I will show you how to take it like a man'.

The defendant was committed for trial at Maidstone Assizes on Wednesday, 24 June, but with Bryant still admitting his guilt, the outcome was a foregone conclusion and the jury returned a Guilty verdict without leaving the box. Asked if he had anything to say, Bryant replied, 'No, it is the correct verdict,' and thanked the judge on passing the death sentence. There was no appeal and Bryant quietly met his end with some dignity on the gallows at Maidstone Gaol.

For Bill Whiting life continued much as before, with him drifting in and out of the occasional casual job and living in squalid bedsit rooms. Yet his tough swagger always seemed able to attract the ladies and he began a relationship in Dover with Rose Wood-bridge. He was soon invited to share her Clarendon Street home, but no sooner had he moved in than he began a relationship with a friend of Rose's, named Phyllis Spiers, who sometimes stayed with the couple.

Phyllis May Spiers was an interesting character who had already packed a lot into her twenty-two years. Born Phyllis Minter in 1916, her parents ran the Radnor Lodging House in the old Folkestone fishing quarter in Radnor Street and at the age of sixteen she began a relationship with Arthur Spiers, who worked at the house. Within a few weeks they were married at Folkestone Register Office

Phyllis Spiers, the victim of Folkestone's Green Scarf Murder in 1938. *Folkestone Herald*

Radnor Street, Folkestone, showing the Radnor Lodging House in the centre, which was run by the Spiers family. Folkestone Library

on 11 April 1932, and nine months later on 25 January 1933 Phyllis gave birth to a daughter.

The new family decided to move to Bexhill-on-Sea in order to make a fresh start, but Phyllis soon realised that a cosy domestic life was not going to suit her outgoing ways. In April 1934 she absconded back to Folkestone, leaving her husband and daughter behind in Bexhill. A poor persons' divorce was subsequently granted to Mr Spiers in November 1937.

Back in Folkestone, Phyllis soon gained a reputation for being 'free with men'; despite living on-and-off with a man named Thomas Butcher for two years. She had another child by Butcher, but as neither of them wished to care for the baby it was put into a Dr Barnado's Home, although occasionally Phyllis did contribute to its upkeep. Butcher eventually tired of his partner's continual dallying with other men, but she soon found solace in the arms of a soldier named Wells. They even lived together for a couple of weeks, but upon the transfer of his regiment to Aldershot Phyllis, already tiring of the relationship, refused to go with him.

However, an attractive young woman like Phyllis Spiers found it easy to attract men during her many visits to the local pubs, and she would occasionally earn some extra money by obliging her admirers with certain favours. Now and then she would try her hand at a more honest occupation, such as a stint as a hotel cleaner during the summer of 1937, but she would soon slip back into her old ways.

Phyllis appeared to hit it off with Whiting because she shared his dishonest traits and penchant for not settling at a permanent address. Lodgings would be sought at various boarding houses in the town, but as soon as she was pressed for the rent Phyllis would pack her meagre possessions into a suitcase and disappear without paying. It was all rather sad how she had allowed her life to descend to this level.

Bill Whiting was another who was always on the move, this time back to Folkestone at 50 Dover Street. Rose Woodbridge had sent him on his way once she had discovered he had been seeing Phyllis behind her back. Yet, as was the case with all the other men she had known, Phyllis was growing tired of Whiting, who she thought of as only a casual acquaintance, and only bothered to meet him occasionally. Nevertheless, when they bumped into each other at around 1.00 p.m. on Monday, 23 May 1938, Phyllis appeared to be in a good mood and suggested they go for a drink at the *Globe* pub. Over a glass of brown ale she even proposed they get married, although Whiting took this as a joke and added he would need to find some steady employment first.

Following their drink, they walked through the town centre into New Street, then along Bradstone Avenue where on the corner with Sussex Road Phyllis spoke briefly to Mrs Nora Laws, one of the landladies to whom she owed money. Phyllis and Whiting then made their way up past the Royal Victoria Hospital to the entrance of the golf club, and then, according to Whiting, back up Cherry Garden Avenue to Cheriton Road, where they parted.

Three days later, on Thursday, 26 May, a sixteen-year-old boy named Kenneth Andrews found the body of a woman hidden by bushes in a coppice at the foot of a hill between Holywell and Caesar's Camp. He ran home as fast as his legs could carry him and told his father, who immediately summoned the police. An examination of the body found the victim was in her early twenties, approximately five foot three inches in height and of slim build with bleached brown hair. She was wearing a dark-green dress with a matching green scarf tied tightly around her neck, a pair of blue shoes and a blue coat covering her body. The police

Cherry Garden Avenue, where it is likely that Bill Whiting and Phyllis Spiers walked together before Phyllis was found murdered beneath the hills in the distance. *Alan F. Taylor*

immediately suspected the body to be that of Phyllis Spiers, whom they knew well, and her ex-husband, who was called upon to identify her, confirmed this.

A full-scale murder investigation was launched and door-to-door enquires were carried out. The local newspapers covered the case extensively and appealed for witnesses. Mrs Laws came forward to say she had seen Phyllis in the company of a man aged between thirty and forty, while Mrs Margaret Wright revealed she had gone shopping with Phyllis on the Monday morning. They had arranged to meet later that day to visit the cinema, but Phyllis never showed up. During the door-to-door enquiries, John Hairbird remembered seeing Phyllis walk past the end of Julian Road (just up the road from the hospital) in the company of a man he knew to be Bill Whiting.

Whiting was brought in for questioning by New Scotland Yard, who had taken over the murder investigation, during the evening of Monday, 30 May. He was questioned extensively for over four hours before signing a statement confessing to the crime. However, on being formally charged with murder, he replied that he was not guilty and had only signed the statement to end his ordeal.

During a visit to the murder site on the day the body was found, Chief Inspector Hollands of Folkestone Police observed that the ground where the body had lain was dry, whereas the coat that had covered it was damp. Because the last dry day had been Monday and it had rained on the three days since, he concluded that the body must have been there since Monday, the last day she was seen, in the company of Bill Whiting.

The Chief Inspector's theory was initially backed-up by the Police Surgeon Dr Barrett, who conducted a full post-mortem of the body on the day it was found. He concluded that Phyllis had died three days earlier, on the Monday, because putrefaction had begun to set in and blowfly eggs had been found in the dead woman's hair. However, by the time of the inquest four days later on 30 May he appeared to have changed his opinion. Now he stated that he had found no evidence of putrefaction and Phyllis had probably died only two days before her body was found. It appears, by all accounts, that Dr Barrett had been taking notice of all the gossip in his surgery, which was saying Phyllis had been seen alive after the Monday, and he began to doubt his own findings!

Fortunately, Dr Bernard Spilsbury, that most eminent of pathologists and forensic scientists, upon whose evidence many of the most notorious murderers of the first half of the twentieth century were convicted, was invited to conduct his own examination of the body. He immediately challenged the findings of Dr Barrett, and added that, following a thorough examination of the body, he had discovered that considerable pressure had been placed on the windpipe. This meant the likely cause of death was manual strangulation, rather than strangulation by the green scarf, which gives the murder its popular title of the 'Green Scarf Murder'. Spilsbury also derived the important conclusion that the murder had taken place on the Monday, due to the hatching of the blowfly eggs. These would not have been laid until putrefaction had started to set in after three days (on the Thursday when the body was found) and the eggs would have needed a further two or three days to hatch, which they did on the Saturday.

Two years on from having helped send his wife's murderer to the scaffold, it was now Whiting's turn to stand trial for murder. Although the odds appeared to be heavily stacked against him, the case was not as clear-cut as that of Bryant. This was because during the trial eleven witnesses came forward claiming to have seen Phyllis Spiers on the Tuesday and Wednesday following her supposed death on the Monday. One of them was a shop assistant in Woolworths, who claimed to have seen Phyllis in the shop on the Wednesday purchasing a roll of greaseproof paper. However, she was clearly mistaken, for although Phyllis had indeed been in the shop that week, it was on the Monday with Mrs Wright, who had purchased the paper.

The testimonies of the other witnesses were just as suspect, and although it seems unlikely that all eleven of them could be wrong, this does appear to be the case. It would seem they either saw Phyllis on an earlier day, mistaken her identity altogether, or wanted to get their names into the newspapers.

However, their testimony was to prove crucial in sowing seeds of doubt in the minds of both the jury and the presiding judge, who emphasised they must acquit Whiting if they harboured any doubts over his guilt. They did, and after two-and-a-half hours of deliberation they found the defendant not guilty and he was free to walk out of the court an innocent man.

But was Bill Whiting really innocent of the murder of Phyllis Spiers? Although he had his supporters, there were many that believed he was a very lucky man who benefited from a bungled police investigation and a certain amount of sympathy over his murdered wife. They say a very different series of events occurred during that fatal afternoon of Monday, 23 May 1938, at odds with what Whiting had claimed. Instead of parting at Cheriton Road, the couple walked up Cherry Garden Avenue to a lonely spot at Caesar's Camp, perhaps for the purposes of sex. Here, Phyllis might have said something to irk that 'wiscous' temper and Whiting strangled her.

Whiting had managed to successfully claim away the presence of the green scarf around the neck of Phyllis by saying he had given it to her sometime previously. However, there was another piece of evidence he could not explain away, and that alone, many have said, should have been enough to convict him. One corner piece of the dark jacket he always wore was found to be missing on examination, and the absent fragment was later found attached to barbed wire close to the murder scene.

Having literally got away with murder, it seems, Bill Whiting finally bowed out of the local newspaper headlines.

CHAPTER 26

The Ghost of R.M. Qualtrough

Sholden, 1939

On the morning of 10 July 1939 Mrs Margaret Jackson was found battered to death in her home at Sholden, just outside Deal. This totally baffling and unsolved case is interesting in that it mirrors in many respects the famous Wallace murder case some eight years previously. Both victims were the wives of devoted husbands who were suspected of the crimes, but were ultimately set free. The two couples were also childless, lived in respectable neighbourhoods and kept themselves to themselves in an outwardly dull existence. Wallace in particular displayed an outward lack of emotion and feeling which made him a rather unsympathetic character. However, whereas a plausible subject is now firmly in the frame for the murder of Mrs Wallace, that of Mrs Jackson is still very much a whodunit.

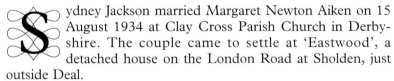 ydney Jackson married Margaret Newton Aiken on 15 August 1934 at Clay Cross Parish Church in Derbyshire. The couple came to settle at 'Eastwood', a detached house on the London Road at Sholden, just outside Deal.

Five years into their marriage, and aged twenty-eight and twenty-six respectively, Sydney and Margaret were still seemingly very much in love. They preferred not to mix with others, although they were both members of the Peardorm Social Club at Betteshanger Colliery, where Sydney had been employed for the past seven years as a wages clerk. He was considered a reliable and conscientious employee and always ensured that 'Carrots', as he liked to call his wife, because of her ginger hair, was given £1 10s housekeeping money per week. The couple enjoyed playing tennis at the social club, but never joined in with any of the social activities. Margaret, in particular, was very shy and reserved, and the only visitors they entertained at home were Sydney's brother and his wife.

To keep her company Margaret had a little dog, which acted as a guard dog for the nervous woman. Upon hearing the slightest

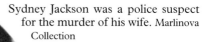

Sydney Jackson was a police suspect for the murder of his wife. Marlinova Collection

noise, the dog would look out of the window and bark at anyone who approached the house.

On the morning of 10 July 1939 Margaret awoke early as was usual. She went out into the garden to chop the wood needed to light the fire in the kitchen so she could do the washing. Outside the front of the house, at around 7.15 a.m., four workmen arrived to tar the pavement and parked their tar boiler, roller and cart on the corner of Sholden New Road. An hour later, the workmen decided to halt for breakfast and, as one of them knew the Jacksons, another (named Osgood) was sent to Eastwood to fetch some water. As he walked up the path to the front door, which was on the right-hand side of the house, the dog saw him and barked, before jumping down from the window-ledge. When Margaret Jackson opened the door the dog rushed at Osgood, who patted the hound on the head. Margaret asked the workman if he wanted hot or cold water before going to fetch it.

Sydney Jackson was upstairs shaving when Osgood called at around 8.20 a.m. Ten minutes later he finished off the last of his breakfast and left his wife finishing hers as he left for work. He kissed her goodbye and then set off on his bicycle for the journey to the colliery. On the way he met a workmate and they cycled together to work.

At 9.50 a.m. the milkman from Steed's called at the house for his money, but most unusually received no answer. He heard the dog barking continuously and thought the pet had the run of the house as the barks varied in volume.

Throughout the rest of the morning, the neighbours later reported, all was quiet at the house, even the dog. Another who used the side footpath that passed by the house also heard nothing.

Mrs Margaret Jackson, victim of the unsolved Sholden murder. Marlinova Collection

Sydney Jackson returned to the house at 1 p.m. and immediately sensed that something was wrong. For a start, his wife was not there as usual to greet him, and she had also not done the washing, which she always started at 9 a.m. Furthermore, the milk money was still with the milk book. The dog was also shut in the front room, which usually only happened when visitors called, and the back door was unlocked. This was most unusual because Mrs Jackson was wary of strangers and had been worried about the presence of tramps in the area.

Feeling distinctly uneasy, Sydney ventured upstairs and in the bedroom he shared with his wife found her lying face downwards and diagonally across the bed. She was naked save for her dress, which had been pulled up to her shoulders and torn, and as he lifted her head saw she had a severe wound. Although her shoulder was warm, there was no sign of life.

Eight years earlier, during the evening of 20 January 1931, William Wallace had returned home to 29 Wolverton Street in the Anfield district of Liverpool to find his wife, Julia, battered to death. Wallace, an insurance salesman for the Prudential, had just returned from a fruitless journey to find an address that was proved not to exist. The saga had begun the previous evening when at 7.15 p.m. a call was made to the Central Chess Club at the City Café asking for Wallace. The caller was told he was not there, but the captain of the club, Samuel Beattie, spoke to him and took the message asking for Wallace to call round to Mr R.M. Qualtrough at 25 Menlove Gardens East the next evening at 7.30 p.m.

The message was passed on to Wallace when he arrived at the

'Eastwood', London Road, Sholden, the scene of the unsolved murder of Margaret Jackson in 1939. Marlinova Collection

club. He expressed bemusement at the name Qualtrough claiming he had never heard of anyone with that name. He also denied knowing a Menlove Gardens East, although he was told it must be near Menlove Avenue. Nevertheless, on the following evening he left the house at 6.45 p.m. and at 7.06 caught a tram to Menlove Avenue. However, he was unable to find Menlove Gardens East, only a Menlove Gardens North, South and West. After a fruitless search, and countless enquires, Wallace returned home to find his wife had been killed. Some money had also been stolen, yet the murderer had been less than thorough, as other money lay untouched.

Sydney Jackson, upon finding his wife's body, ran over to 'Ingleside', the home of the Doubledays, who had a telephone because of Mr Doubleday's job as a rating officer for the district. Unable to fully comprehend what had happened, he asked Mrs Doubleday to phone for the police and a doctor. After doing this, she volunteered to return to Eastwood with Mr Jackson and took over a bottle of sal volatile to help calm him down.

Back at the house, a police sergeant arrived and Mrs Doubleday took him up to the bedroom while Sydney Jackson remained

Mrs Julia Wallace, whose murder in Liverpool in 1931 was mirrored in many respects by the Jackson killing eight years later. Marlinova Collection

in the kitchen. Taking note that the body was largely naked and the underclothing (which lay torn on the floor with an apron) had been removed, the police officer immediately deduced a sexual motive for the attack. However, there was no sign of any struggle or disturbance around the house, and robbery was unlikely to have been the motive as a ladies' gold watch and a 6d coin in the bedroom had not been touched.

Curiously, a stepladder was left placed on the landing as if to retrieve something from the loft, and the lights had been left on in the bathroom and on the landing to provide lighting. Yet Margaret had always hated going up into the loft and insisted that her husband do it. Amongst the items found in the loft were some suitcases.

Doctor Milne arrived shortly after the police and examined the body of Margaret Jackson. Upon returning downstairs he was asked by Sydney Jackson if his wife was dead, to which the doctor replied, 'Yes'.

The post-mortem on Mrs Jackson was carried out by the eminent pathologist Sir Bernard Spilsbury in company with two

William Wallace, who was tried for the murder of his wife, Julia. Marlinova Collection

The body of Julia Wallace lies battered to death on 20 January 1931 at her home at 29 Wolverton Street, Liverpool. Marlinova Collection

local doctors. Both Spilsbury and the Jacksons' own doctor, Dr Fraser of Eastry, calculated that Margaret had died around twenty to thirty minutes after eating her breakfast as the food had not been digested. As breakfast took place between 8 and 8.30 a.m. the probable time of death was between 8.45 and 9 a.m. A hard, blunt instrument with a comparatively small striking surface had been used to knock Mrs Jackson unconscious before she was manually strangled. Bruises found on the thighs and groin were result of an attempted rape, while another on the face was caused by a punch. A further bruise on the back of the head occurred after the victim had banged it on a hard surface.

Both Sydney Jackson and William Wallace were naturally police suspects, as husbands usually are when a married woman is murdered. Wallace's quirky 'Qualtrough' story quickly put him in the frame, especially after the police discovered that 'Qualtrough' had made the call to the City Café from a phone box just a few minutes' walk from Wolverton Street. Furthermore, there was no sign of any forced entry into the house. The last person to have seen Mrs Wallace alive was a milk boy, who claimed to have called at around 6.45 p.m. (the time Wallace had said he left the house to catch the tram to Menlove Avenue). Yet the police, without any definite proof, claimed that the boy had called about ten minutes earlier and then Wallace killed his wife before leaving the house. He had conducted the elaborate Qualtrough plan to provide himself with an alibi. However, the police's own tests showed that Wallace must have left the house no later than 6.49 to catch the tram (and even that timing was suspect for Wallace had only one kidney and was a slow mover, and therefore he would have surely missed the tram if he had left the house that late). So if the milk boy's timing was correct, Wallace would have had all of four minutes to kill his wife and clean himself up!

Sydney Jackson, however, was not arrested until a full month after his wife's murder: on 11 August 1939 when two police officers approached him outside Snowdon Colliery with the words 'You know who we are'. He was taken to the police station at Sandwich, where he was charged with the murder of his wife.

The court hearing opened at Canterbury on 29 August 1939 when Sir Bernard Spilsbury gave a detailed account of his post-mortem findings. He reiterated that Mrs Jackson must have died soon after eating her breakfast as in the case of sudden death the body stops digesting food. The police contended that because of the short timespan in which the murder must have taken place the killer must have been Sydney Jackson, before he set off for work at 8.30 a.m.

While awaiting his hearing, Mr Jackson was housed in Brixton Prison. However, the magistrates decided that no convincing case could be made that he had murdered his wife, and he was set free. To escape from all the local gossip and publicity, Sydney Jackson went to stay with his brother.

On the other hand, William Wallace was not so fortunate. He was tried and convicted of his wife's murder, although the sentence was soon quashed. Yet, Wallace never got over the loss of his beloved Julia and on 26 February 1933 he died of a broken heart aged fifty-four.

The real killer of Julia Wallace remained a mystery for many years and was much debated over, with some still claiming that William Wallace was the murderer. However, in recent years, a strong suspect has come to light, although he had passed away before he could be fully investigated. Richard Gordon Parry was a young petty criminal who knew the Wallaces well. He had worked with William Wallace as a Prudential agent and had often visited the couple at their home. Wallace himself had pointed the finger for his wife's murder at Parry, but at the time the suspect appeared to have a cast-iron alibi (supplied by his girlfriend, who later revealed that it was false).

Parry certainly had motives to carry out the crime. He was always short of money and knew Wallace's collecting routine, which meant on Tuesday evenings he always had a large amount of cash to pay in the next day. Parry was also aware that Wallace had a chess game to play at the City Café on the Monday evening as his amateur dramatic classes were held at the same venue. Furthermore, Parry held a grudge against Wallace for reporting him to Prudential for fiddling the books. Fifty years after the crime, it was uncovered that on the night of the murder Parry had gone to a garage to have his car hosed down and the cleaner had found a bloodstained glove in the vehicle.

There was perhaps one other motive Parry may have had to kill Julia Wallace: one that shocked William Wallace and all who knew Julia to the core. Parry had revealed that he often visited Julia when her husband was out at work to sing with her as she played the piano, and hinted there may have possibly been some kind of relationship between them. Perhaps beneath that shy, middle-class, but rather dull, demeanour Julia Wallace had craved some love and excitement in her life? We shall never know.

A strong suspect for the murder of Margaret Jackson, however, has yet to be unearthed, although it possible that she too may have been killed by an unknown lover who had pepped-up her otherwise mundane life. Another in the frame is a neighbour who was on friendly terms with the Jacksons and often called round. That perhaps explains why the back door had been left unlocked and the dog, who was very protective of its mistress, had not barked. Could the neighbour have also returned to the house later that morning to shut the dog in the front room?

Perhaps one of the tramps that Margaret was so worried about could have carried out the murder? Sydney Jackson expressed the opinion that a tramp was the killer, and had entered the house intent on robbery but upon discovering Mrs Jackson had killed her to keep her quiet. However, if this was the case, why wasn't any of the money stolen? Furthermore, if a tramp had entered the property from the side alley why didn't the hedge show any signs of being pushed through?

The four workmen were all interviewed and cleared, and they supported Sydney Jackson's claim that he had left the house for work at 8.30 a.m. His journey to work was corroborated by the cycle rider and a witness at a bus stop. The police argued that he could have carried out the murder immediately before he left for work, but Jackson's defence claimed that it would have been a curious time for him to have committed the crime, especially with the workmen outside.

The two murders remain officially unsolved, and although equally intriguing in their own right, one of them (the Wallace case) continues to be the subject of much debate while the Jackson case is all but forgotten. William Wallace and Sydney Jackson went to their graves as free men, but with a clear conscience as well? That is for you to decide.

CHAPTER 27

The Supplementary Horror Show

Dover, 1941

As the bombs and shells rained down on 'Hellfire Corner' during 1941, the Plaza Cinema remained open to provide some welcome relaxation for the hard-pressed citizens and military personnel of war-torn Dover. Opened on 1 July 1929, the Plaza seated 1,200 and was noted for its sliding roof. As the last patrons left the evening performance of 'Arise My Love' on the night of 3 July 1941, little did they realise that another drama, of the most horrible kind, was only just beginning.

Following the end of the nightly show the manager of the Plaza, fifty-year-old George Roberts, liked nothing better than to relax with a drink in the Friends' Social Club opposite the cinema. Roberts had recently been transferred from the Regent Cinema, Chatham and to save the journey to his home in Second Avenue, Gillingham took to sleeping in the Plaza. While he was at the social club, he left the cinema in the hands of his secretary, Ellen Tolputt, and night watchman Sidney Williams, who came on duty after the last performance had ended at 9.30 p.m. One of his duties was to watch out for any incendiaries that fell on the Metropole Buildings, where the cinema was situated. Miss Tolputt left the building at 10.30 p.m. when Roberts returned from the social club.

Sidney Williams finished his shift when the cleaners arrived at 8 a.m. One of them, Mrs Foot, was cleaning the female staff changing room when she noticed a dark stain on the tiled floor, which someone had tried to wipe off. She also spotted that a photo frame and vase had been moved from their usual place on the windowsill to a shelf.

Another of the cleaners, Mrs Southwell, was cleaning the manager's office when she noticed a stain on the carpet. She thought that perhaps George Roberts had been sick, and so she cleaned the stain with disinfectant. The manager's rolled-up mattresses evidently had not been slept in and his two towels were

The programme at the Plaza Cinema, Dover, for the week commencing 29 June 1941. 'Arise My Love' was shown the night cinema manager George Roberts was murdered by one of his employees. *Dover Express*

missing. A third cleaner, Mrs Roberts, was dusting the office when she saw that her namesake had unusually left his keys on the desk. However, none of the cleaners suspected that anything was particularly wrong and so nothing was reported.

At 10.30 a.m. Miss Tolputt arrived on duty and was surprised to find that her manager was not in his office. Furthermore he had left his keys on the desk, which included the safe key. She decided to check the safe just in case anyone had been tempted to look inside, and to her horror found that the float money (around £3) and one of the blue canvas money bags were missing.

A search of the cinema failed to locate Mr Roberts so Miss Tolputt telephoned the Granada Cinema, which was part of the same ABC chain as the Plaza. An assistant manager came round to the Plaza and along with Miss Tolputt checked the contents of the safe, where they discovered that in fact over £30 (kept in the

The site of the Plaza Cinema in the Metropole Buildings, Dover pictured *c.* 1910. Bob Hollingsbee

canvas bag) was missing. The senior manager for the two cinemas, Sidney Sale, was contacted and after looking around the Plaza concluded that Roberts had probably run off with the cash.

The police were called and DI Datlen and DC Thain of Dover CID arrived at the Plaza. The cleaned-up stains in the female changing room and manager's office were pointed out to them, as were the displaced items from the windowsill in the changing room. As the detectives looked out of the changing-room window they noticed a reddish mark in the cemented basement area. They decided to have a closer look and armed with torches searched the little-used workshop and small rooms housed in the basement. In a recess in one of the rooms, the torchlight illuminated the battered body of George Roberts. Upon closer examination it was found that his head had been completely smashed in by three blows, one of them causing the top of the head to completely split open.

With a clear case of murder on their hands, the Dover Police called in their Scotland Yard counterparts, who sent Super-intendent William Rawlings and Detective Sergeant Marshall to Dover. A further search of the basement uncovered a blood-

The home of Leslie Hammond at 85 Buckland Avenue, Dover. Marlinova Collection

stained axe, which was obviously the murder weapon. The missing money from the safe led the detectives to presume robbery was the motive for the crime. However, with few signs of a break-in and no fingerprints, the police began to suspect that a member of staff, or at least someone who knew the cinema well, was involved.

All of the staff were brought in for questioning and the night watchman Sidney Williams in particular was subject to some intense grilling. Nevertheless, he stuck to his story that he had heard or seen nothing, and with all the other staff appearing to have cast-iron alibis the investigation ground to a halt.

Yet upon rereading the statements of the staff, Rawlings began to have suspicions about the account provided by eighteen-year-old Leslie Walter Hammond, one of the four projectionists at the

Plaza, who lived at 85 Buckland Avenue, Dover. Hammond stated that, after the end of the evening's show, he had stood talking to his brother outside the cinema until 9.55 p.m. Then, to fill in the sixty-five minutes before his firewatching duty at the Midland Bank began at eleven o'clock, he had gone for a walk around the town. However, when the police walked the route Hammond had described, they found it took them only forty minutes.

On 21 July 1941 Hammond was brought in to account for the missing twenty-one minutes in his statement. In addition, they had discovered that he had not actually arrived at the bank until 11.30 p.m., so now there was in fact a 51-minute discrepancy in his timing. Upon being asked to explain this, the clearly nervous young man hesitated for a full five minutes before replying with a vague answer about funny feelings in his head. He also admitted that he may have gone back into the cinema after the end of the last film.

Hammond was then asked to provide another statement, which became a full confession to the murder. Hammond's motive for the crime was indeed robbery (to supplement his meagre weekly wage of £1 12s 6d), which he had planned only on the morning of the murder. After talking to his brother outside the Plaza, Hammond had not gone for his walk but had returned inside the cinema. He waited for Roberts to come back from the social club and then went to fetch the axe he had hidden earlier in the switch room. As Roberts walked through the vestibule Hammond sneaked up behind him and struck him with the axe. As the manager slumped to the floor another blow struck him in the face. As blood poured from the wounds, the murderer tied a tablecloth around the head of his victim and dragged the body into the female changing room. Hammond had planned to hide the body in the basement but he decided that the route through the auditorium was too risky as there was a chance Sidney Williams would see him. The only other way to get the body to the basement was to throw it out of the ladies' changing room, a drop of twelve feet, which Hammond, with considerable strength, managed to do. He then made his way through the cinema to the basement and dragged the body through the workshop into one of the small rooms. He knew the rooms were not used and therefore presumed the body would never be discovered.

Upon making his way back to the manager's office Hammond noticed Roberts's overcoat so he quickly ran down to the basement to drape it over the body. Returning to the office he grabbed two towels and used them to wash the floors of the vestibule and ladies' changing rooms. The axe was then disposed of by throwing it through the ladies' changing-room window into one of the basement rooms below. Hammond then robbed the safe and left the keys on the desk before making his way to the men's changing room, where he was violently sick. After cleaning himself up, the young man quietly left the building and made his way to the bank.

The murderer then revealed to the police where he had hidden the money. A bundle of notes totalling £18 was found hidden in a parcel in the outside lavatory at his home, and more of the money was concealed inside a cistern in a public lavatory at Charlton Green. When Hammond was strip-searched a bag of silver coins was found inside his underpants. The bag was marked with 'Plaza Cinema, Dover' and 'RW', which was the initials of the Plaza's cashier, Rose Williams.

Leslie Hammond was charged with the murder of George Roberts and in September 1941 was sent for trial at the Old Bailey. Although it was an open-and-shut case, the defence argued that the statement Hammond had provided was not admissible because it was made under duress. The jury was asked to withdraw while the defence counsel interviewed the three police officers who had taken the statement. A lengthy debate then followed on the legality of the statement until the Judge, Mr Justice Cassels, ruled that it had been made voluntarily.

Found guilty, Hammond was sentenced to death. An appeal was rejected, but the murderer's father, a member of the Auxiliary Fire Service, organised a petition for a reprieve on account of his son's age. This public support was perhaps influential in the sentence being commuted to life imprisonment on the eve of Hammond's execution.

Perhaps the reprieve was only right, for Hammond's undoubted immaturity left its mark all over this bungled murder, carried out just for £30 in cash. The ghost of his victim is said to still haunt the old cinema, which in 1960 was converted into a bingo hall.

CHAPTER 28

A Cruel Night Out

Folkestone, 1943

Folkestone was not a particularly pleasant place to be in 1943. With its position close to France and the German army, the town was subject to regular bouts of bombing and shelling and its population dwindled during the war from 45,000 to just 9,000. However, those that remained behind tried to make the best of it, particularly a vivacious and pretty eighteen-year-old like Caroline Ellen Trayler.

Caroline lived with her parents, Mr and Mrs Stapleton, at 3 Sussex Road; although, in fact, she was a married woman, having wed 22-year-old Edgar Trayler some six months previously. Though Edgar was away on active service in North Africa and to keep herself occupied Caroline obtained a part-time job as an usherette at the Central Cinema.

Whilst no doubt missing her husband, Caroline predictably became bored with the nights spent in at her parents' house. Like any young woman of her age, she craved excitement, so after the end of the evening show at the cinema on Whit Sunday, 13 June 1943, and with it still being light, Caroline decided to go for a drink. However, ignoring the well-known pubs in the centre of town (where, perhaps, she was worried about being seen) she made for the *Mechanics Arms*, tucked away in St John's Street. Rather unusually for a woman, she ordered half a pint of bitter and sat herself down in a corner of the bar. Being on her own, a pretty girl like Caroline was bound to attract the attention of men, and sure enough two soldiers named Leckey and Knight began eyeing her up. Caroline, her ego suitably flattered, shyly smiled back.

Gunner Dennis Leckey, a burly 24-year-old Mancunian, was married with two children, but fancying his chances with Caroline, soon engaged her in conversation. Within a short time they left the pub together, probably on the pretext of Leckey walking Caroline home, and were seen strolling down war-

Caroline Ellen Trayler, cruelly murdered by Dennis Edmund Leckey in Foord Road, Folkestone on 13 June 1943. *Folkestone Herald*

ravaged Clarence Street, apparently arm-in-arm. They continued into Bradstone Road and then New Street before turning into Foord Road. There was still a little daylight left when they were seen entering an empty shop on the corner of Foord Road and Devon Road, just a hundred yards or so from Caroline's home in Sussex Road.

Inside the shop, the couple engaged in some heavy petting before Caroline lay down on the dusty floor in preparation for sex. However, perhaps still conscious of being a married woman,

The home of Caroline Trayler at 3 Sussex Road, Folkestone. Marlinova Collection

or realising she was in the company of a sexual sadist, she changed her mind as Leckey was about to begin the sexual act. Sadly for Caroline, the frustrated Leckey was aroused to the point of no return and was in no mood to change his mind. He proceeded to brutally rape the unfortunate woman before strangling the life out of her. But that was not all, for this truly evil brute then defiled the lifeless body even further by wrenching the dead woman's engagement and wedding rings from her fingers. Making sure the coast was clear, he then quietly left the shop, leaving behind

The *Mechanics Arms* pub, where Caroline Trayler fatefully met Dennis Leckey.
Folkestone Library

Caroline Trayler was murdered by Dennis Leckey in this shop at the corner of
Foord Road and Devon Road (seen here in 1951). Alan F. Taylor

Dennis Leckey, the
soldier who got away
with the murder of
Caroline Trayler.
Marlinova Collection

the pitiful figure of poor, and fatally naïve, Caroline Trayler
sprawling in the darkness and dust of the otherwise empty shop.

The wretched soldier decided not to return to his camp on the
transport provided but to make his own way back, arriving at
around 1.30 a.m. Upon being reprimanded for being late, he
offered the excuse he had helped a WAAF with her suitcases.

Meanwhile, Mr and Mrs Stapleton, upon finding Caroline had
failed to return home, had informed the police. They organised a
search party who began checking empty houses and shops, along
with Folkestone's numerous bombsites.

Back at camp, Leckey made what should have been a fatal
mistake, which later became the linchpin of the case for the
prosecution. Two days after the murder, on Tuesday, 15 June, he
asked a friend if he had heard of Caroline's murder, yet at that

stage she was presumed to be just missing. Her body was not to
be discovered until two days later, so how did Leckey know she
had been murdered?

Upon finding the body, Folkestone Police quickly called in
Scotland Yard. The local force was still somewhat in disarray after
a major scandal which had forced the resignation of the Chief
Constable. In addition a sergeant and five constables had all
resigned from the force after it was discovered they had been
shop-breaking while on night duty and storing the stolen property.
An ex-policeman who was also involved was sentenced to nine
months' imprisonment.

The Yard called in pathologist Professor Keith Simpson to
examine the body. He found:

> *She had been strangled, and there had been rough sexual intercourse
> shortly before. Bruising of the vagina and thighs signified inter-
> course of some violence, though it had not necessarily been opposed
> when it began. Indeed, it seemed more probable that she had at first
> consented, for the outer sides of her calves were dirtied by contact
> with the floor, as if she had been lying with her legs flat on the floor
> and wide apart. From her injuries I deduced that she had resisted
> an attempt to grasp her neck from in front, and then had turned or
> been turned on her face and strangled from behind. It had been very
> quick, only about twenty to thirty seconds, perhaps because her face
> was buried in her left arm. I found six dark hairs, in striking
> contrast to her own auburn body hairs, stuck to her thighs. One of
> her fingernails was torn, probably through clawing at her assailant.
> I took scrapings from under the nail and found one short rust-brown
> wool fibre freshly torn away from the material to which it had
> belonged.*

In the meantime, Leckey, having realised his mistake of 15 June,
got jumpy and left the barracks the following day on a forged leave
slip. He also stole several pay books and a quantity of cash, which
enabled him to fund a brief visit to his family in Manchester.
Having told them he was on embarkation leave before being sent
overseas, he then travelled back down to London, where he
lodged at the *City of Quebec Hotel*. However, by this time, Leckey's
desertion from the army had made him a prime suspect in the
Caroline Trayler murder case and his picture was in the newspapers. At the hotel, an American airman recognised him from
one of the photographs and informed the police. They took
Leckey to Marylebone Police Station and, after initial questioning,
Folkestone Police were alerted. Two detectives travelled up from

Folkestone to London, and following further questioning formally charged Dennis Edmund Leckey with the murder of Caroline Ellen Trayler. The accused was taken to Folkestone and held on remand while awaiting trial for this hideous crime.

Keith Simpson found plenty of evidence to connect Leckey to the murder:

> *The trail led to gunner Dennis Leckey, who had gone absent the day after the body was found. Ten days later he was apprehended walking in London, and PC Briggs, who arrested him, recognised him as the man wanted by Folkestone Police. After being formally cautioned he exercised his right to make a statement until he had obtained the advice of a solicitor; and, of course, the solicitor advised him to say nothing.*
>
> *The police brought me samples of Leckey's body hairs, which I compared with the six hairs found stuck to Caroline's thighs. I found them identical in character, colour and form. Meanwhile Dr Davidson, then Director of the Metropolitan Police Laboratory, had found an auburn hair identical with Caroline's clinging to Leckey's uniform trouser leg. The word 'identical' did not mean the hairs had necessarily come from the same person, only that they could have. That is the most one can ever say about hairs. Identical hairs are not compelling evidence like identical fingerprints for they carry so much less detail.* [This was before the use of DNA finger-printing, of course.]
>
> *The police also brought me Leckey's clothing, and I found that the fibre from under Caroline's fingernail was 'identical' with one of the component fibres from which his khaki shirt had been made. Again, that was far from saying the fibre must have come from Leckey's shirt, for this was standard army issue. Identical fibres could have been found in thousands of other soldiers' shirts. But the evidence of the hairs and the fibres together would of course strongly corroborate any circumstantial evidence that might be brought to connect Leckey with the crime: this kind of evidence always has a strong influence on a jury.*

The trial began on 21 September 1943 at the Old Bailey. Leckey refused to say a word except to plead not guilty. The evidence against him, particularly the forensic, was overwhelming. The prosecuting counsel, Mr Flower, also pressed home that Leckey and Caroline were seen leaving the *Mechanics Arms* by Bombardier Knight, and several passers-by had seen them enter the empty shop. The theft of the pay books and cash was also used to damn Leckey.

The defence counsel, led by Mr J. Caswell, could offer little in the way of excuse, although they claimed Leckey had left the girl alive at 10.30 p.m. It appeared to be an open-and-shut case, and Judge Justice Singleton appeared to agree in his summing up. Three times he stated that Leckey's silence was not the action of an innocent man, and because of his silence in court, the jury could only arrive at one verdict. They did (within half an hour): guilty. Judge Singleton duly donned the black cap and sentenced Leckey to hang.

However, not surprisingly, the defence counsel immediately appealed against the verdict because of the bias of Judge Singleton. They claimed he should not have advocated that Leckey was guilty of the crime just because he remained silent throughout the trial. The appeal was heard in November 1943 and was successful. Leckey was a free man.

Around the time Leckey was being freed, Edgar Trayler turned up at his in-laws' house, probably in the company of an army escort. He had known nothing of his wife's murder until at least a month after it had happened. After being refused compassionate leave, he had apparently deserted from his army unit and somehow had found his way back to England.

So a plainly guilty man was saved from the hangman's noose by to the sloppiness of a judge and the integrity of British justice. Dennis Leckey was a very lucky man. If he is still alive, I wonder if his mind ever wanders back to wartime Folkestone, that dark, dingy shop and poor Caroline Trayler.

Bibliography

Primary Sources

Folkestone Chronicle
Folkestone Express
Folkestone Herald
Folkestone News
Folkestone Observer
Dover Express
Dover Telegraph
Hythe Reporter
PRO MEP03/803 Phyllis Spiers murder

Secondary Sources

Aspin, John and Alan Greenhalgh. *Frances Kidder: The Last Woman to be Hanged in Public* (authors n/d)

Bishop, Bill. *Kent Crimes and Disasters* (Geerings 1993)

Easdown, Martin and Linda Sage. *Rain, Wreck & Ruin: Disaster and Misfortune in Folkestone, Sandgate, Seabrook and Cheriton* (Marlin Publications 1997)

Easdown, Martin and Linda Sage. *The Path to Journey's End* (Marlin Publications 2001)

Easdown, Martin and Linda Sage. *Jack the Ripper in a Seaside Town* (Marlinova 2002)

Easdown, Martin and Linda Sage. *Hythe: A History* (Phillimore 2004)

George, Michael & Martin. *Coast of Conflict* (SB Publications 2004)

Ingleton, Roy. *The Gentlemen at War: Policing Britain 1939–45* (Cranborne Publications 1994)

Ingleton, Roy. *Policing Kent 1800–2000* (Phillimore 2002)

Lane, Brian. *The Murder Club Guide to South-East England* (Harrap 1988)

Laurence, John. *Seaside Crimes* (Sampson, Low & Marston n/d)

MacDougall, Philip. *Murder & Mystery in Kent* (Robert Hale 1995)

Ogley, Bob. *Kent 1800–1899: A Chronicle of the Nineteenth Century* (Froglets Publications 2003)

Rayner, Denise. *Fire, Flood & Sudden Death in Old Hythe* (Hythe Civic Society 1996)

Roy, John and Tony Thompson. *Picture Palaces Remembered* (Glenton 1987)

Bygone Kent (various issues)

Index